Shayne Kawalilak
Charles ·········

don't be the
WEAKEST
link

Don't Be the Weakest Link

Don't Be the Weakest Link

Shayne Kawalilak ◉
Charles ●●●●●●●●●● ◈

don't be the
WEAKEST
link

How to Protect Your Personal
Information in a Digital World

Kawali
Publishing

Don't Be the Weakest Link

Quantity sales and special discounts are available to organizations, associations, book clubs, and others. For details, contact the publisher below.

Book Design: Shayne Kawalilak
Cover Design: Design by Kat
Editor: Ger Hennessy

First edition 2025

10 9 8 7 6 5 4 3 2

ISBN   978-0-9937440-6-8 (audio book)
ISBN   978-0-9937440-5-1 (digital book)
ISBN   978-0-9937440-4-4 (hardcover)
ISBN   978-0-9937440-3-7 (paperback)
ISBN   978-1-0691917-0-0 (large font)
ISBN   978-1-0691917-1-7 (Bionic Reading® for ADHD)
ISBN   978-1-0691917-2-4 (digital Bionic Reading® for ADHD)
ISBN   978-1-0691917-3-1 (hardcover Bionic Reading® for ADHD)

Kawali
Publishing

www.KawaliPublishing.com

Don't Be the Weakest Link

DEDICATION

This book is dedicated to Chelsey, Chantell, Ryan, Casandra, Raimond, Randal, Rembrandt, Russel, and Cydnee. I should add the fiancés and spouses that have been a part of this journey as well. Whether they supported me or one of my kids, it gave me more time to focus my attention on a computer screen and pile of paper. That would add Dion, Matt, Helen, Josh, and Amelia to this list.

These children have seen it all with their crazy father. This is an apology and explanation for the number of times I passed on family poker night, sitting around a campfire, playing with grandkids, and overall being present for the past year.

I suppose it's been a 5-year process but for this past year, as we got closer to the book launch, my children whose primary love language was 'quality time' have been wholly dependent on their mother. That hasn't been acceptable, but it is what it is.

I appreciate them all for their patience and hope that they read this book, learn from the lessons, and spread the teachings to my six grandchildren as well as the many more that are bound to arrive in the future.

I love you all dearly.

My wife has a whole page at the back of the book, so I have left her out of the list above, except for the part where she carried these nine humans in her belly for 6.75 years of our 37 years of togetherness... kinda.

If Charles was willing to let me share whether he had a family he would undoubtedly thank his wife and children if they existed. Since I am not allowed to corroborate or deny the existence of said family, we will say that Charles is thankful to those who stood by him during this crazy adventure.

Don't Be the Weakest Link

Table of Contents

INTRODUCTION

Prepare **yourself** for **a rollercoaster of emotion** and **knowledge** pulled from the **passionate lessons** of two **professional geeks**. **Combined, Charles** and **Shayne** have over half a century of experience with technology, and their perspectives will provide you with both unique and often opposing opinions. You will see a common belief in everything they stand for...

Your personal security and online privacy need to be protected!

Charles and **Shayne** are both **professional geeks** who have been full-time **employees** and **contractors; they have worked for small** and large **businesses; they have worked for governments** and non-profits; and they have commuted a few minutes for work and to other countries occasionally.

**Shayne is going to write most of this book from his perspective
and professional experiences, but he will also write about Charles's
perspective and show where it is similar and where it varies. It will
become clear that not all IT Professionals think the same way.**

IT: Information Technology

Information Technology (IT) is a set of related fields that encompass
computer systems, software, programming languages, and data and
information processing and storage.

**The purpose of this book is to be educational and enjoyable, but
it also needs to scare you. Having fun might keep you reading, and
learning might keep you interested, but without being scared by the
world around you, will you be engaged?**

**If you are searching for serious technical directions for locking
down a computer or web browser, or if you want to erase your digital
footprint and disappear to everyone but the FBI, then keep searching.
There are better books out there. There will be some outstanding
books recommended throughout the coming chapters and in the
Additional Reading List section at the back of the book.**

FBI: Federal Bureau of Investigation

The domestic intelligence and security service of the United States
and its principal federal law enforcement agency.

**If you are looking for simple steps to make your online data more
secure, then you have come to the right place. Charles and Shayne
both believe that everyone should take protection of their data more
seriously. One is more solemn about it than the other, but they are
both professionals with the same goal: to spread information that will
make the internet a safer place for everyone.**

> Goal: to spread information that will make the internet a safer place
> for everyone.

WHY DOESN'T CHARLES HAVE A LAST NAME

Charles didn't want to be a credited author of this book. **He hasn't written much of it at all. By saying** "not much", **I me**an not a single word.

Charles has, however, totally changed the direc**tion of the book. He has made crea**tive **contrib**utions **that cannot be overs**tated. **Without him, this book would not exist in its curr**ent form, and **may**be not at all.

Don't Be the Weakest Link would probably have been educational without him. It would have had an abundance of facts and data. It probably would have been fun. But the book would not have blended the fun into education like it has now.

After some convincing, Charles finally allowed Shayne to give him credit **on the cover, but on the condi**tion **of exclu**ding **his last name. At first, Shayne thought this was crazy. How could a cover include just an author's first name? It would look like his co-author was Prince or Madonna. Katarina sugge**sted **the privacy blur and Shayne never looked back. She was wor**th **every penny as a cover desi**gner.

> We will include videos, going into further details about the production of this book, on the website at www.DontBeTheWeakestLink.com or www.DBTWL.com if you prefer the short version.

Charles and Shayne have been friends for **over twenty-five yea**rs, **but that is not how Charles got dragged into this project.**

THE BEGINNING

Companies and organizations **have been paying Shayne to come do presenta**tions **for their employ**ees **or mem**bers **for many yea**rs. **Shayne teaches how to protect their pers**onal **information online. The benefits then flow to the organiz**ations **when atten**dees who take better care of their personal information will have the knowledge and tools to be better stewards of the business's data.

Shayne realized he could only reach so many people through personal meetings in boardrooms. He needed to put his lessons into the hands of people he would never meet face to face. He needed to write a book.

With decades of experience as a writer and with technology, Shayne thought he would take a week off work to turn his presentation into a wonderfully educational book. After 40 hours of devoted time, he had a rough outline and one solid chapter. This would not be the simple project he had planned for.

Taking the week off was a great start, but in the end, Shayne had a short story at best, and it was not captivating. The book was missing the hook. It was missing the stolen cheese[1]… the five languages[2]… the 12 rules[3]… the seven habits[4]… the five laws[5]… it was missing the poor father[6]! Where was that hook that would make people remember this book, that would make them want to read it in the first place and then recommend it to a friend?

Shayne has given every one of those books above as gifts (Who Stole My Cheese, The Five Love Languages, 12 Rules for Life, 7 Habits of Highly Effective People, The Richest Man in Babylon, and Rich Dad, Poor Dad). Some of them, many times over. He was several chapters into the writing of this book, still knowing that there was no

---

[1] Who Moved My Cheese?
http://footnote1.dbtwl.com
[2] The Five Love Languages
http://footnote2.dbtwl.com
[3] 12 Rules for Life
http://footnote3.dbtwl.com
[4] The 7 Habits of Highly Effective People
http://footnote4.dbtwl.com
[5] The Richest Man in Babylon
http://footnote5.dbtwl.com
[6] Rich Dad, Poor Dad
http://footnote6.dbtwl.com

hook that would allow someone to enjoy <u>Don't Be the Weakest Link</u> to its full potential.

He outlined several more chapters and got to writing. The book clearly needed a lot more research than Shayne had initially planned, and he assumed the hook would appear to him in the middle of the research. That was when Shayne asked Charles if he could bounce the first few chapters off him, since he thought the two of them were so similar.

The input that Charles offered was not what Shayne expected.

Shayne and Charles had been discussing work-related projects for decades. This was nothing new. The book was new though. Charles was looking at it for the first time, and evidently, with a different perspective.

Shayne came to realize that Charles, after decades of friendship, had many secrets. They did NOT agree on everything. He knew Charles would add insight to the facts and information in the book, but he did not expect that he would help produce the hook that Shayne was so gravely searching for.

THE WEAKEST LINK SCALE

Throughout this book, there will be references to the Weakest Link Scale (the hook that Shayne was looking for), which is a way to measure how individuals understand and respond to the threats to their personal information. You will hear about how Charles and Shayne compare to one another.

Many times, you will see how they are so similar that they could be brothers. Other times, you will see how they couldn't be more different from one another... a lot like different brothers. Using the brother analogy might not be working here.

The Weakest Link Scale is a combination of two Rankings:

```
┌─────────────────────────────────────────────────────┐
│        Your Knowledge Ranking: A  B  C  D  F          │
└─────────────────────────────────────────────────────┘
```

Your **Knowledge Ranking** is between an **A** and an **F**, and just like in school, you want to aim for the lower letter.

```
┌─────────────────────────────────────────────────────┐
│        Your Response Ranking: 1  2  3  4  5           │
└─────────────────────────────────────────────────────┘
```

Your **Response Ranking** scores how securely you react to your knowledge on a scale of 1 to 5 where 1 is living in the woods and having no online footprint at all, and 5 is tired of resetting the **Netflix** password because it has been compromised so often.

As an **A4**, **Shayne** understands how his data can be compromised, and he takes measures to prevent it from getting too far away. He also prevents data he didn't want to share from becoming public knowledge. If you think of your private information as money, **Shayne** gives his money to many people online, but he works hard to limit who is taking his money and how much they are receiving.

Charles protects his information much more diligently as an **A2**. Being an **A**, he is just as knowledgeable as **Shayne**, but where **Shayne** has a huge online presence, **Charles** has chosen a path that restricts the number of people who even know who he is online. **Charles** doesn't lock himself away in a cabin (that would make him a 1), but he prioritizes the security of his digital information in a much more significant manner than a 4.

Using the money analogy, **Charles** does not work as hard to limit where his money goes so much as he works hard to limit the number of people who even know he has money.

For now, considering what you think you know about online security, what would you think your **Knowledge Ranking** is? Remember that **A** means you know everything you need to know to protect you and your data online, and an **F** means you do not know what to protect or how to protect it.

Now decide where you are on the **Response Ranking**. A 1 is you, locked in a cabin, and a 5 is you give little thought to passwords except to keep them easy, and you may only have a couple that you use over and over.

We will delve more into the Weakest Link Scale in **Chapter 1: Find Your Weakness**.

THE OUTCOME

Charles is not one of those guys who steals internet access from his neighbors or has his water bill come to an alias, but you will see how he protects his personal information in a much more determined manner than Shayne does.

If you ever post a picture of Charles online, he will promptly ask you to remove it. He would never willingly give his personal information to Facebook, Google, or the NSA (National Security Agency). He believes in everything in this book and follows most of the security recommendations religiously.

Shayne also believes the principles in this book and follows most of the recommendations... using the word "religiously" would be tantamount to a lie. His online life is an open book. If you can't find some information about him on social media, then you can find it on a blog or in a video. Shayne does not have many secrets from his online communities.

One of the clearest distinctions between these two authors is that Charles uses his knowledge to limit the way he interacts with the world, and Shayne uses that same knowledge to affect how he secures the way he interacts with the world. Shayne realizes that by following his desires, he inherently has more risk, so there is extra work required of him. Charles finds it easier, and more secure, to simply not make those same choices by avoiding the security risks.

Neither of them is wrong, but Charles is more secure and less likely to be hacked, no matter the effort that Shayne is willing to invest.

These facts are undisputed.

YOUR CHOICES

Charles and Shayne have both dealt with security issues for users at various companies throughout their careers. The one constant that they both agree on with security is that most people simply don't do enough of anything.

This book opens your eyes to some vulnerabilities that you might be unknowingly exposing yourself to. It will help you secure your personal information before you lose it. You will learn how your data ends up in the hands of people you didn't give it to, and hopefully, help you prevent it from going there in the future.

Throughout the book, you might see a constant struggle to word these ideas in common terms. For years Shayne has stated one of his most valuable skills is the ability to translate "geekanese", or "Nerdwegian" to my European friends, into English. Transcribing their conversations word for word, would prevent the intended readers of this book from enjoying it. What would be the point of you reading a book that was all about DNS, AES, IPSEC, blah blah blah?

Instead, they have worked tirelessly to create something that you could understand without having "professional geek" spelled out with ludicrous acronyms behind your name. Not only will you not need a computer science degree or five years of experience in the field, but you won't even need to know how to program the clock on your microwave.

All you will need is a name and an email address to read and play along with this book. No email address? That simply means your email address has never experienced a hack. You are already halfway to securing yourself, though it's a mystery how you found this book without an email address or social media account. There must be some great marketing behind this project, to say the least.

AFTER READING THIS BOOK

The authors wrote <u>Don't Be the Weakest Link</u> hoping you would give it away after you read it, but you should probably read it more than once. After you have read through the book, gauge how much you learned from the first pass. If your Knowledge Ranking didn't improve much, then either you didn't pay enough attention, or you were already an A.

If you feel you jumped from an F to a B however, give the book another read to make sure you are a B. What happens often when we learn a lot in a short time is that we overestimate how much we have retained.

You may feel like you just drank from a fire hose, which will get you really wet, but probably will not quench your thirst. Now that you have all this additional knowledge, a second reading will help you understand a whole lot more of what you are learning.

Shayne and Charles do not want to be at fault for leading lambs to slaughter by giving you a false sense of security. They would much rather you finish this book with a healthy fear of potential threats and the knowledge to confront them.

To prevent that false sense of security, and to allow some of the more technical parts to really sink in now that you have implemented them in your life, they invite you to read through the book again before you give it away. Or, as an alternative, buy a second copy of the book, give away your copy, and read the second one for the first time. That suggestion might have come from the publisher... or Shayne's wife.

We also recommend giving away your first copy because an unread book is 70% more likely to never be opened. That's right, you are much more likely to read a book that already has dog-eared pages and wrinkles all over because you subconsciously know that the person who gifted it to you has already read and approved the content.

THE BOOK ANATOMY

The primary aim of each chapter will be to educate and involve you more with your personal security. This will make you a better employer, employee, parent, child, sibling, friend, and person overall. It will give you the tools to go out and share the education you gained with others and make the online world a safer place.

By learning just how vulnerable we are, you might take this new knowledge and secure your information just a little more tomorrow, and Charles and Shayne will have successfully accomplished a lofty aspiration.

The bulk of the writing will just be Charles and Shayne talking about the things they wish that every client and end user knew about protecting their personal information. Interspersed throughout the chapters will be a few special areas that should be both entertaining and educational.

STORY TIME

Each chapter will include at least one Story Time section. Some of these stories are going to be personal reflections from Shayne or Charles. Some stories will be ripped from headlines that you may remember reading about yourself. They may be gentle reminders about the topic of the chapter, but they may be frightening tales of how real the threat of personal data intrusion can be.

TTT - TIME TRAVEL TIPS

Because technology changes so rapidly, Shayne and Charles will use the power of the internet to help keep the topics of this book up to date. Go to the book's website at www.DBTWL.com or www.DontBeTheWeakestLink.com, and then click on "The Book". There will be a list of chapters where you can find all the Time Travel Tips. The site will update the Time Travel Tips every year so long as people are going to the site... or until Shayne can no longer type.

Don't forget to sign up for the site's newsletter so you can receive updates when the Time Travel Tips are revised.

One of their most sincere hopes is that the website will allow them to avoid releasing a new edition of this book every year. Technology changes so quickly that without a method of updating you online, the book would become less relevant sooner than they would want to publish an updated version.

Throughout the book, the Time Travel Tips will be noted with a line starting with "TTT".

PLAY ALONG

You will also find a Play Along section at the end of each chapter, which will give you some tasks to follow along with in your personal life.

You can find these online as well, by going to the book's website at www.DBTWL.com. These short missions will take you to places you might never have gone without direction, but they each aim to be educational or enjoyable, or possibly both.

Kudos To You

Shayne used to skip the Introduction and foreword in books. He always thought they were a waste of time, but he is now reading them constantly and cannot believe how insightful they are to the pages that follow.

Kudos to you if you are already at a place that has you reading the "entire" book. You are leaps ahead of where Shayne was just a few years ago.

If you didn't read the **Introduction** before starting the book… kudos to you for coming back to it.

CHAPTER 1: FIND YOUR WEAKNESS

We have no interest in your IQ. You could read this book and get a lot out of it, whether you are a certified genius or dumb as a sack of hammers. We are going to assume you are somewhere in the middle.

Before we get too far into the book, we need to assess where you are on the **Knowledge Ranking** on the **Weakest Link Scale**. This would have been one of those things that would have confused me because I would have skipped the **Introduction**. Hopefully, you read the **Introduction** and know exactly what we're talking about.

Once you know where you are on the **Knowledge Ranking**, we will go through some aspects of technology to determine where your weaknesses are and work on limiting their impact on your life. Our goal is to help you educate yourself so that you aren't the weakest link in protecting your personal information or the information you might be responsible for at work or elsewhere.

By reading this book, you will hopefully change your strategies and tactics about how you use the internet, but our deepest goal is to help you change your mindset so that you approach the internet with a clearer understanding of what threats are out there. At that point, it is up to you to decide how you interact with those threats.

AT HOME

The thought of living in today's world without technology seems absurd to most of us. In a college course I was told to analyze my bank statement and review my spending. My discretionary money went overwhelmingly to things that did not exist 50, 30, even 20 years earlier. Some technology seems to take forever to get into the mainstream or even get a foothold in the marketplace, while other technology seems to appear everywhere overnight.

The lithium-ion battery has taken over the world today. They are in all our electronics and even our cars now. I can't even find a nickel-cadmium (Ni-Cad) battery for any of my power tools anymore. I still remember buying those big, bulky Ni-Cad batteries and probably still have some in the garage somewhere. It's hard to believe that lithium-ion batteries were invented in 1985. I was still in high school. How did it take so long for lithium-ion batteries to displace the older technology?

When do you think the invention of electronic cigarettes took place? You are probably wrong. Probably off by a few decades. They are over 60 years old. That's right. The electronic cigarette entered the market as a smoking alternative in 1963. Most people guess some year in the 21st century, making them typically off by 40 years.

Looking at my credit card statement today, so much of what I purchase with my discretionary money would be things that were invented much more recently.

Some **technology** is **exploding** so **fast** that it is **outpacing** our **ability** to **design** and **implement** security **practices** around it. The **newer technology** seems much **more invasive**. Unlike **a microwave** or **rechargeable battery**, social **media** and **cell phones interrupt** our very **existence sometimes**. For the **record**, the **microwave** was **commercially available** in 1967, **making** it over 55 **years** old **as well**.

Think of the **internet bill** you **pay every** month (**World Wide Web invented** in 1990). **We** use **that service** for **everything** from **checking email** (**Gmail invented** in 2004, **Office365 invented** in 2011) to our social **media accounts** (**LinkedIn** 2003, **Facebook** 2003, **Twitter** 2006).

I use the **internet** to **stream movies** from **Netflix** (1997 but **started streaming** in **Canada only** in 2010) and **Amazon streaming** (2006 but **didn't hit Canada** until 2016). I **use that internet connection** to surf the **web with browsers** like **Firefox** (2002) and **Chrome** (2008). **Many** of **my searches** use **Google** (1998), **DuckDuckGo** (2008), or **Brave** (2021). I **could** go on and on, but **most** of the **applications, companies,** and **solutions** we **will talk** about **did not exist** much **over 20 years ago**.

AT WORK

Almost every one of **those things** listed **provides a security issue** in the **workplace** as well. **Yes, even services** like **YouTube** (2005) **pop** up in **workplaces** all **over**. A **good technology department deals with many security issues**, but **every employee has a role** to **play, whether** you **are answering** the **phones** or **responding** to **emails**. As **an employee**, the **simplest thing** you **could** do **for your company's** security is to **read** and **follow your cyber-security** or **security policy...** and **this book**.

What do **you mean** you **don't have a policy?**

Many small businesses with less than 20 employees don't need a policy. If you don't think your company needs an HR policy, then you probably don't need an IT or cyber security policy. Most companies with any policies, should have an IT policy.

Once you have these policies in place, follow them. You might not understand why you are doing everything you are doing, but it is important that there are standards that all users and equipment adhere to. This reminds me to ask you to be nice to your IT professionals. They work hard and probably have more than a few plates spinning on sticks right now.

Businesses also must deal with an additional issue arising from employees being asked to do things they would never consider when they were in their private world. Considering these new environments, and how to react to them, is a key component in securing the office from intrusion. This could be as simple as learning which emails to respond to and how to respond to them effectively. It could be as simple as understanding who has physical access to the location.

At home, you have a well-defined list of people who can access your space, especially after hours or in your absence. In the office, however, that line gets blurred. It's more confusing when others are changing the list, often without your knowledge.

As an IT professional, I regularly perform security assessments. I often do a physical walk through to see how difficult it is to have someone escort me to the server room. It is likely not surprising to hear that I rarely encounter any obstacles and sometimes convince someone to retrieve a key for a locked door.

EMPLOYEES

So how do you prevent yourself from being the weakest link in the security of your company? The simplest thing you can do is learn how to protect yourself better in your personal life. The lessons that you learn, and the habits that you create in your personal life, will translate cleanly into a corporate environment.

One thing I have been doing for years is selling my time to organizations who pay me to present on the topics in this book. These presentations typically range from 45 minutes to a couple of hours.

You would be correct to assume that there are probably a few things in this jumble of words that are not covered in my presentations, which is why I also offer full-day workshops... which still don't include everything in this book.

Why do you think organizations pay me to speak to their teams? If paying me a little today will save a day of downtime in the future, or a potential loss of data or client confidence, then what they pay me will be an insignificant cost for a considerable value. I could charge $10,000 for that one-hour session and if it saved one system outage, it would still be worth it for most small or medium businesses.

Imagine the value for a larger company. Which reminds me, I should probably raise my speaking prices.

STORY TIME – IBI GROUP

During one of our editing sessions, I read this title and Charles interrupted me, "Wait, you are actually going to tell them where you worked?"

"Yep... because I am not a 2", was my snappy response.

The year is 2003. I worked full time for IBI Group, a large architectural and engineering firm with about 2000 employees. An architect called me to his office. All his images are gone. They actually are not all gone, they still look like they are there, but they all now have a new file extension which means instead of ending with .JPG files which usually open in a graphics program, they now all end with .VBS which is a script that runs the infection again if you open it.

It then sends itself to everyone in the infected computer's email address list, which then spreads the infection to everyone else at that company. Most people are expecting it to be a photo, so they double-click and infect their computer and try to send hundreds of emails through a new contact list. It was a vicious circle.

From an IT perspective, it would have been much better if the images had been deleted.

Because that user had shared drives mapped from a central server, we lost about 450,000 photos in a few seconds. It was not a great day for the IT department. We were restoring images from backups until almost midnight that evening. That user never had his pictures restored to his laptop because they weren't being backed up.

When investigating how and why the virus was introduced to the computer we found that the user was sitting at his desk when he received an email about an election in the United States and he instantly thought it was suspect. He was about to delete it when another person who was in the office asked him to open it because she was an American and was a little more curious… and a lot less cautious.

Lesson learned.

WHAT INFO IS AVAILABLE?

What kind of personal information would you be comfortable sharing with anyone online? What information would you not want out in the public domain? Let's have a look at the personal details that get stolen most often.

- **Real name**

- **Username**

- **Email address**

- **Password**

- **Password hints (or security questions)**

- **Geographic location**

- **Physical address (that's your home address)**

- **IP Address (your computer's address)**

- **Date of birth**

- **Gender**

- **Website activity (that's a list of websites that you visit)**

- **Job title**

Let's take a serious look at what these pieces of data are worth to you and to the people who sell them.

Real Name

Your real name probably is not that important. You give it to people all the time. On the flip side, if a stranger walked up to you on the street and asked what your last name was, would you give it to them? Clearly, Charles would not be pleased about his name being exposed on the internet. I, on the other hand, wouldn't care if my name were on a billboard in Times Square, so long as it was spelled correctly.

If this is the first time that you have heard Charles's name, you probably pulled a "Shayne" and skipped the **Introduction**. You really need to pop back and read through it quickly. We will chat more about him in a few pages as well.

Username

Your username is quite ubiquitous. You probably use the same one on many sites. I use "ShayneNeal" frequently. It often means nothing at all. On sites where you connect with other people, (X, Facebook, LinkedIn, MySpace, Instagram, Gradfinder, etc.) many people use their real name for a username, which then moves it up the ranks into a more significant privacy concern.

Email Address

The email address is another one that you give away often but also holds personal value, and while you might not mind sharing it everywhere, nobody appreciates that it leads to more spam emails every day. We also attribute a different value to our work account, **IAmAnAdult@BigCompany.com** and the personal email we setup in high school, **HandsomeRob@freemail.com**.

Password

There should be no doubt about the privacy concerns of your password being exposed. The entire purpose of the password is to be the private key that allows you to authenticate to a service in such a way that you are confident nobody else is logging in as you.

> The password is the lynchpin of securing your online personal information.

Password Hints

Your password hints or secure hints (also include security questions) could be more severe losses than your password because there is a chance that your passwords are different between websites and applications, but your mother's maiden name is always the same, as was the make of your first car. Those things simply don't change. Maybe they should, but we will talk about that in **Chapter 6: Security 2.0**.

Geographical Location

Your **geographical location** could be a serious loss if you were in the **witness protection program**, but it might still be more of a privacy violation to everyone else than losing your physical address. Your geographical location is not the address you tell people you live at or get your mail delivered; it is the physical location that you logged into. With cell phone capabilities, you may be sharing your exact location with people and companies that you never intended to share it with.

Physical Address

Your physical address could be a box number or a simple lie if you never plan to get mail from the site you are signing up to. It is much easier to use a false physical address than a false geographical location.

IP Address

The IP address comes from your Internet Service Provider (ISP) and might change often. While it isn't critical to your privacy because it typically takes a court order to have the ISP tie that address to your name, the IP address gives hackers a gateway point at which to direct future attacks and this might lead to much more serious issues in your future.

ISP: Internet Service Provider

A company that provides internet access to its customers, enabling them to connect to the internet, access web content, conduct online activities, and communicate with others for a fee.

If you want to keep your identity more hidden, keep in mind that many ISPs and third parties share your information without court orders or warrants. The Supreme Court in Canada recently ruled that the IP address can be used to invade someone's privacy. It is

now **illegal** to **disc**lose **a** pers**on's** IP addre**ss** **with**out **a** cour**t** ord**er** or
warrant [7] (**tha**t's in **Can**ada).

Date of Birth

If the **world** knew **my** date of **bir**th, I couldn't care le**ss**. **Peo**ple
post it on social med**ia** and many offices send out **birt**hday **car**ds, so
it isn't the most crit**ical** pie**ce** of da**ta**.

On the flip si**de**, the **government** in **Can**ada **thi**nks it is **cruc**ial, and
if some**one** is stea**ling** **y**our **iden**tity, it is one of the key **compo**nents
of that the**ft**. **Y**ou should prob**ably** **n**ot adver**tise** th**is** date
every**where**, even if it means **n**ot being wis**hed** **a happy** birt**hday** by
people you don't care eno**ugh** to **ta**lk to in the re**al world**.

Gender

What can I say ab**out** some**thing** that society **n**ow tel**ls** us is fl**uid**.
It can change more often than your ema**il address** and it is **illegal** to
ask you ab**out** it in many **places**. I have **n**o care **whats**oever if the
world thinks they kn**ow** what gen**der** I was wh**en** I signed u**p** on so**me**
websi**te** 12 **years** a**go**.

Website Activity

Website **activity** is **a data**set who**se** val**ue** is **subj**ective. **Mo**st
people **really** would **n**ot mi**nd** if the **world** knew what their brow**sing**
history was, but then there are some **people** that would pay to keep it
priv**ate**. Tho**se** people prob**ably** sho**uld** have done something mo**re** to
prot**ect** their online security before**hand** but, **hindsight**, rig**ht?**

These **people** **are goi**ng to love **Chap**ter 5: **The Inform**ation
Superhighway.

---

[7] Canadian Privacy Law
http://footnote7.dbtwl.com

Job Title

Your job title is one of those pieces of data that is quite unobtrusive. Does anyone care if some stranger knows what your job title is? Agreed. This one probably won't be mentioned again in this book.

THE WEAKEST LINK SCALE

Now that you know what types of personal data might float around out there, you need to decide where you fit on the Weakest Link Scale.

The Weakest Link Scale consists of two variables...

1. The Knowledge Ranking (A – B – C – D – F)
2. The Response Ranking (1 – 2 – 3 – 4 – 5)

Your Knowledge Ranking is a lettered scale reminiscent of grade-school where F is a "fail"... you know nothing about who has your data or how to protect it. An A is the top mark... meaning you understand all the aspects of securing your personal information online. B, C, and D will be somewhere in between.

For the future discussions in this book, we assume that Charles and I are both an A. We have both been professional geeks for over 25 years. Charles prefers Information Technology Professional, but geek is much easier to type.

Your Response Ranking is a number scale from 1 to 5 where a 5 is someone who simply doesn't care if their accounts get hacked and they do nothing to prevent it. A 1 is someone who almost completely limits their online interactions. Their real name and address do not exist on the internet. They struggle with the idea of filing taxes under a fake name, but their phone and utilities get billed to a PO Box or an alias. They have encrypted every email they have ever sent.

Many people who have a Response Ranking of 5 are there because they simply aren't aware of how risky their activities are. Most people who have a Response Ranking of 5, but are also a D or F on the Knowledge Ranking, would believe they were a 3 simply because they do not know what they do not know about online threats.

This book aims to increase your knowledge so that you can carry out your responses in a more secure manner, rather than changing the way you respond to your knowledge.

If I were to just pick a number, I would say that I was a 4 and Charles was a 2. It's an arbitrary number that Charles and I have discussed profusely during the writing of this book.

During your journey, going through these chapters, you will realize just how different Charles and I are.

Shayne... A4

Charles... A2

Just in case you skipped the Introduction, this would be a great opportunity to go back and see how the Weakest Link Scale came into being. To summarize again, Charles and I have both been professional geeks for decades and between us, we have well over 50 years of experience with the technology we discuss in this book.

Over that time, Charles and I have taught thousands of people how to be more secure online. We have both had to deal with data compromises and both had personal experience with our own information being lost or stolen.

DATA BREACHES

Data breaches range from single users to hundreds of millions of victims. The typical breach today probably affects around 500,000 users. It is reminiscent of the data loss that we saw in January 2017 when a retail company, Sephora, lost 780,000 customer accounts, including email address, name, gender, date of birth, ethnicity, and other personal information. This breach affected users in Southeast Asia, Australia, and New Zealand.

Larger breaches might not be as common, but in 2008, Myspace suffered a data breach that exposed 360 million accounts. That breach included email addresses, usernames, and what are basically the first ten characters of the password. Since most users still think that an 8-character password is secure enough, hundreds of millions of accounts probably lost their password in its entirety.

These 100M+ breaches are getting more common. My biggest concern about the Myspace breach was that it wasn't announced for 8 years, and Myspace didn't break the news. Someone who saw the data for sale on the internet exposed it.

I am not sure whether Myspace was hoping to hide the breach or whether they were unaware that it ever occurred. I am also not sure which one is a better option. Neither is acceptable when you consider the data was supposedly being protected by IT professionals. This was not a mom-and-pop corner store. This was one of the first social media monsters. Even if you don't know who Myspace is or was, you don't have to be a mathematician to understand the scale of losing details on 360 million users.

In 2022, before Elon Musk bought Twitter, that platform only had 229 million active monthly users. Some reports show that after rebranding to X, removing substantial fake computer accounts (BOTS) and half their employees, the social media platform in 2024 had over 600 million monthly active users (MAU).[8]

---

[8] X (formerly Twitter) usage numbers
http://footnote8.dbtwl.com

It is no surprise that through many searches[9], Charles's email address appears in exactly zero online breaches. Mine appears in at least nine.

EDIT: since we started writing, Charles now appears in four breeches and mine is in ~~14~~ ~~16~~ 18.

Let's be honest about these increased numbers. These numbers should surprise nobody. We have used these email addresses in newsletters and online subscription sites for decades. The law of averages says that some of these sites will be hacked, and we will lose our information.

What we should take from this is not that I know less about security than Charles, but that we take drastically different approaches toward sharing and protecting our information.

We should also take note that no matter where you sit on the Knowledge Ranking, you are probably going to lose some information if you put it online.

In the Play Along section, you will determine how many breaches have included your email address. Try this with your personal and work email addresses to check if either has experienced any breaches.

Hackers compromise personal emails much more often than work emails. If your job requires you to sign up on many online sites or if you've been at your job for a long time, your account may have already been breached. Due to concentrated phishing attacks, company emails are being compromised with a much higher frequency in recent years.

Remember that Charles and I have both lost data to hacks. Being compromised isn't a reflection of your knowledge, nor is it

---

[9] Compromise searches are currently done through HaveIBeenPwned.com but if this changes, the link on DBTWL.com/Tools will be modified to keep you current and this book relevant.

necessarily bad. It does not mean that you are at further risk or that you are insecure, but it absolutely means that you have a reason to pay attention to some lessons in this book.

These breaches were not your fault, they are the responsibility of the companies that were holding your personal information.

Some things that you are about to learn may be easy for you to grasp and significantly increase your security. Some things may be much more difficult to implement and have a lower return. As you are reading through the myriad of things that you can do to prevent yourself from being the weakest link in securing your information, I want you to consider something that a friend in Saskatchewan says all the time...

> "Is the juice worth the squeeze?"
>
> ~ Scott Cheston

If the effort to make a change in your life is way more intense than the reward it may bring, then consider that the juice might not be worth the squeeze and move on to another lesson.

PLAY ALONG

Welcome to the first chapter's Play Along section. All Play Along sections can be found with updated instructions by going to the book's website at www.DontBeTheWeakestLink.com or www.DBTWL.com and click on "The Book" and then the chapter you are looking for.

Task 1-1   Have You Been Hacked?

www.dbtwl.com/tools

You can go to the book's website at www.DBTWL.com and click on tools or type the website address above. Then click on the link under "Hacked?", then enter your email address in the search bar. If you have been included in breaches, you can scroll to the bottom and read about them and click on any links in the descriptions to read more details if you feel geeky enough.

You should then take a few minutes and go to each of those websites to see if you still have an account and, if so, immediately change your password. We will talk more about this in the coming chapters as well.

After spending some time online determining if your personal information has already been compromised, we are going to perform a few simple searches to help you determine your current position on the Weakest Link Scale.

Task 1-2 Google Name Search

The first search will be going to www.google.com and typing in your name. If you have a common name, you will find this less useful and might have to add your middle name, your workplace, or your home city. If you have a name like mine, you are golden. This will help explain the difference in why I place myself a few away from Charles on the Response Ranking.

My name is as unique as they come. A quick search brings up dozens of websites with my name from geek stuff like Spiceworks, Microsoft TechNet, and Plantronics; as a volunteer with Scouts Canada, Search and Rescue, our local children's festival; as a father, husband, and unlikely politician; in newspapers, Facebook, LinkedIn, and Twitter (and now X); and as an outspoken person in blogs and videos.

A search for Charles's full name brings up nothing. Add his middle name and scroll through five pages... nada. If I add his employer though, I strike pay-dirt! Actually, I only get one hit, and it is a third party indexing his name, employer, and office number. I would put a screenshot here, but I am sure Charles will have it removed long before this book is published. Because he is a 2. That is what they do.

EDIT: Charles had the company remove the link within weeks of realizing it was there.

Task 1-3 Google Image Search

Now we will get off the beaten path a bit and talk about pictures. Charles would not be pleased to see his picture on the internet, and he will not be disappointed because I could not find one. I could not find a secondary photo, which would be a picture of his child or a sport team he coached with his name on the webpage.

It is possible that Charles has never actually told me his real name and the person I know might not be a real person. That would explain a lot. We will have to confirm that he isn't in witness protection before publishing this book.

With your name still in the search bar on the Google page, click the word "Images". You will see all the images that Google has tagged with your name. In my search, some images are not of me. If you have enough tags or have an active YouTube channel, you might find similar results.

If you don't see any pictures of you, try Shayne Kawalilak. There should be a few of those.

Now to show you the differences in your search terms, try my favorite poet, "Randall McNair". You will see a lot of pictures of a lot of people with McNair as a last name, but not many of my favorite poet. Apparently, he isn't everyone's favorite... yet.

Now add the word "poet" behind his name and hit enter. Suddenly "Randall McNair poet" fills the page with photos of Randall as well as his books. I imagine by the end of 2025, the searches that readers of this book perform will start to skew the search results. I may have to add a different name here if Randall gets too famous.

I will make sure there is a screenshot of my search with my results on the website under "The Book" and Chapter 1.

You should go through the pictures of yourself and confirm that they are all truly you or tagged correctly. It is also a great way to find out if an ex posted photos of you somewhere... at which point you might need a lawyer - not anything Charles or I can help with.

_____

_____

_____

_____

_____

_____

_____

_____

CHAPTER 2: PASSWORDS ARE STUPID

Passwords are the foundation **of your security. Are you buil**ding str**ong foundat**ions?

Everything **you do onl**ine **seems to nee**d **a password. For years, the** dom**inant bel**ief, **and one you are pr**oba**bly famil**iar with, **was the idea** th**at all passw**ords **should be at lea**st **8-chara**cters **long and use two or** **three of the four character-typ**es. **Although a popular bel**ief, **this has** **been at the root of so many compro**mises.

THE PASSWORD'S TIME IS PAST

First off, **I pre**fer 15 **or more characters as a minim**um. **I also don't** **prom**ote **passwords at all and haven't for over** 20 **years. I prom**ote **passph**rases **over passwords for a few reas**ons.

I love our 7 children!

That was my password for several years for my laptop login. It was still my password well into my wife's ninth pregnancy. It is over 20 characters long and includes all four character-types.

1. **Lower**case letters

2. **Upper**case letters

3. **Numb**ers

4. Special **characters**

This password was quite hard to hack, and still is, except that I have told thousands of people that I used to use it. Once this book is published, that number is going to rise much faster. I hope so at any rate.

Using a passphrase instead of a password, not only makes guessing or hacking your password infinitely more difficult, but it also makes it much easier to remember than something of even half the length and half the complexity.

Passphrases are easier to type and remember because typing full sentences is what we do all the time. #Rft&6zS is not something we type often, and it forces us to type slower. "I love my 2 cats!" is much simpler to remember; much easier to type, making it harder to see as you are typing faster; and it is 17-characters long, making it challenging to crack.

I instructed a password tool to create a password using two dictionary words and capital letters. I then used another tool to determine the time it would take to crack the password using a Brute-Force attack which is basically guessing extremely fast but starting with a long list of the most popular passwords.

Brute Force Attack

A brute-force attack consists of an attacker submitting many passwords or passphrases with the hope of eventually guessing correctly.

PleaseTango - 21 **hours to crack**

So far as passwords go, this is unacceptable. It would be better to add a number or symbol, but we can see that this password would probably take 21 hours to crack. This number is a broad estimate based on technology guessing 100 trillion guesses per second with full local access to the system being hacked.

Assuming that the database or file has been downloaded locally to the hacking computer eliminates all security you might hope slows them down like locking permanently or for a length of time after a number of unsuccessful login attempts.

How important are the number of characters and the character types in reality? If we add one letter to "PleaseTango" we see a decent jump in crack time.

PleaseTangox – 45 **days to crack**

But see what happens if we changed the "x" to a zero and still have the 12-character password but use 3-character types...

PleaseTango0 - 1 **year to crack**

It went up significantly because you added ten additional characters to the algorithm, so the number of guesses has to add that additional 10 guesses to all 12-character spaces.

*Please*Tango# - 45.7 **years**

The special character clearly adds a level of difficulty to the password because the time required to hack it went from 1 year to 45 years simply by swapping the number for a symbol. We don't even have the number any longer. We still only have 3-character types in this password.

This jump happens because there are far more special characters than numbers, which is why I don't tell people to use 3 of the 4-character types. I always suggest using all four of them.

Now let's try it with all four character-types by swapping the "o" with a zero...

*Please*Tang0# - 16,500 **years**

With that same number of characters as Please Tangox (12), but using all four character-types rather than just two, the hack time goes from 45 days to 16,500 years.

I hope you see the value of using all four character-types. Even if computers were 1000 times more powerful, you still have 16 years if you were using all four character-types.

Using all four character-types in a password is critical. There are 26 uppercase and lowercase letters and 10 numbers. There are 33 special characters on most keyboards. By not including special characters, you are removing the largest variety of the four character-types.

Using all four allows each character to be one of 95 various options. You want to use the largest variety of characters to restrict the simplest hacking tools that would compromise your accounts.

To truly to see the value of combining length and complexity with ease of remembering, see what happens when we use a passphrase...

PASSPHRASE

I love our 7 children! - 1 **hund**red **mill**ion **trill**ion **cent**uries (**that is** 22 **zer**os)

That **would look outsta**nding **writ**ten **out**... **it would take a whop**ping 10 **sexti**llion (10,000,000,000,000,000,000,000) **yea**rs **to** crack. **That is quite clo**se **to the num**ber **of grai**ns **of sand on the** planet. **That's a lot of years.** [10]

At this point, do we care if computers **get** 1000 **or even** 1,000,000 **times fas**ter?

Every **space cou**nts **as a spec**ial **chara**cter **and add**s **to the len**gth **of the passw**ord **witho**ut **making it any more diffi**cult **to reme**mber. **Typ**ing **spaces in sent**ences **is eas**ier **to reme**mber **becau**se **it is norma**lly **how we type in our regu**lar **life.**

Not only is it easier **to reme**mber, **but you will type it fas**ter, **mak**ing **it more diffi**cult **for someone to catch your pass**word **look**ing **over your shou**lder.

Keeping **in mind that there are many websites and compa**nies **that still prohi**bit **spaces, and some prohi**bit **passwo**rds **over** 12-**chara**cters, **these are typic**ally **sites that have mino**r **conseq**uences **to being compro**mised.

In my opinion, **use a pass**word **that is a passp**hrase **and make it at lea**st 20 **to** 30 **chara**cters **long. Using** 15 **chara**cters **is the abso**lute **min**imum. **Char**les **agrees with me comple**tely **in this rega**rd.

From **this point on, any time you see the word "passw**ord", **know that we mean "passph**rase". **We mean a minim**um **of** 15 **chara**cters **but recom**mend 20 **plus. We mean all four chara**cter **types all the time, for every single web**site **and serv**ice **that you use.**

---

[10] How many grains of sand
http://footnote10.dbtwl.com

A REAL-WORLD STUDY

An **Imperva** report studied 32 million passwords captured from a rockyou.com database compromise in 2009 and it showed interesting habits for people.[11] This study is more accurate than most you will read about because most require people to answer questions, and most people don't choose to opt into surveys. The ones that opt in choose their answers carefully, or they outright lie.

This study required no input from users. Hackers leaked the compromised database with all the usernames and passwords. Here are some results:

- 30% had a password of six or less characters
- Nearly 50% of passwords used sequential characters
- The most popular password was "123456"
- Five of the top 10 passwords were "12345", "123456", "1234567", "12345678", "123456789", totaling a full 72% of the top 10 passwords and 15% of all passwords.

Did you hear that?

15% of all the passwords were simple sequential numbers. As a professional geek who understands the horrible password habits of people, even I was shocked by this revelation. Three out of every 20 people simply ran their fingers across the numbers on their keyboard to log in. Would you leave your home or car unlocked 15% of the time. Who does that?

The resulting suggestions from the study included using passphrases instead of passwords but their approach is archaic. It also included a suggestion to force scheduled password changes and

---

[11] Imperva Study
http://footnote11.dbtwl.com

the importance of having a password with a minimum of eight characters.

Remember that I do not suggest 8-character passwords. I require 15-character passwords and I suggest 20 to 30-character passwords.

The insecurity in the report conclusions may be the reason that Imperva has removed the report from their site. It will be available on our website though, at www.DBTWL.com under The Book and Chapter 2.

THE DEVIL IS IN THE DEFAULT

Now I am going to tell you about one huge security threat that the world is just now coming to grips with, even though it has been obvious to professional geeks forever: the default password.

There was a day when most ISP routers had the same default password, and the homeowner rarely changed it. Most of us pay Telus, Rogers, Verizon, Quest, AT&T or some similar company for internet services. Those companies supply a box and show you a small booklet with your password for accessing the device and accessing your wireless network. Still today, the vast majority of homeowners never change these passwords.

While it is not as serious a threat as it used to be, you should still make a habit of changing all passwords that you have control over. This includes your internet router (the device that the wires go into that your ISP provided). This is the box that you have to unplug when your internet signal dies during a huge sporting event or during the last ten minutes of a great movie.

This also includes your home security system, small appliances, robot vacuum, speakers, refrigerator, smart TV, game console, and even your doorbell. New devices that connect to the internet are being added to your home all the time, but so many of them don't give you the ability to modify the username or password. This means that if someone could see that device from the internet, they could probably find a tool to authenticate to it and use it without your knowledge.

It only takes a moment to put "TV camera hacked" into a search engine to see what I mean. How many people do you think have had their TV streaming video to the internet without their knowledge? It is a significantly larger number than you would imagine. Most didn't even know their TV had a camera or a microphone. Yes, your TV probably has a microphone and/or a camera if it was manufactured after 2010.

I can't imagine someone creating a device and calling it "smart", as in "smart TV", without giving it a webpage for an end user to log in and reset the admin username and password.

You should also be concerned about all the other devices in the list plus anything else. There are many sites online that stream hacked security cameras, nursery cameras, and other household devices. Most of these cameras are not hacked, they are simply logged into using the default username and password.

When it comes to passwords, use this simple rule of thumb... never use the default password and even change the default username if you can. If it takes a year to guess the password, but you have also changed the username to something other than "admin", imagine the complexity of that math problem for the hacker.

> Never use the default password and change the default username if possible.

AN OLD FIGHT IS GAINING FANS

This is going to be a contentious topic. Many IT professionals still promote regularly scheduled mandatory password changes. Even as recently as 2023, I have worked with large companies specializing in IT security, where mandatory password changes are the status quo.

That **Imperva** study of the rockyou.com hack concluded with a suggestion to IT Administrators to "employ a password change policy". They clarified that this policy could be triggered "by time or when suspicion for a compromise arises". After reading the report several times, I concluded they intended to trigger the policy by time and to interrupt that regular schedule if something suspicious happens.

If something suspicious happens, I am 100% in favor of resetting your password.

I have not been a fan of scheduled password changes since they were made popular by Microsoft over 20 years ago and I still fight against them at every opportunity. While I understand it seems more secure to make a change every few months, does it make sense if you have a great password like…

I love my 65 Galaxy 500 ragtop!

That was one of my email passwords for years. For the record, it would take 65.53 trillion trillion trillion centuries to crack that password.

Why would you want to force someone to change a great password?

As it is, it will not be easily compromised. If nobody ever saw you type it, and your computer is not compromised in other manners, then it is probably as secure as it can be.

If you are forced to change it every few months, one of three things will probably happen…

1. You will make it simpler to remember,
2. You will make it repetitive or reuse another site's password, or
3. You will write it down.

Telling people to stop asking users to change their passwords on a schedule used to get me into a lot of heated debates, but they are getting rarer each year. I have not forced regular password changes on anyone since 2003. If your password is complex, and follows the rules above, the most secure action is to leave it alone until you think it might be compromised. I have some passwords that have not changed in over a decade.

More and more today I am talking to people who agree with me on this security protocol. Even Microsoft started agreeing with me in 2023 when they published new password policy recommendations[12]. I was convinced of the inherent insecurity of this practice right after making wholesale password changes in a workplace around 2002. This is a common practice with corporate networks, where they require specific password policies which force users to change passwords on a predetermined schedule.

I was going to everyone's desk to assist with the changes, and I saw so many passwords on corkboards, or a list under a desk calendar or keyboard, or that prevalent hacking tool, the sticky note.

If people must remember new passwords every three months, they will just document them in insecure manners, which totally defeats the whole point of changing the password.

There is another reason to stop changing your email password, but we will discuss that one in Chapter 8: A Fresh Can of Spam.

I will tell you that if you are an IT Professional and you are still implementing automated password reset policies with your users, you are propagating one of the most significant security threats that exist today. Feel free to tell your IT manager that I said so too. I would

---

[12] Microsoft365 Policy
http://footnote12.dbtwl.com

enjoy the conversation. Tell them to read past the <u>Red Flags section</u> in <u>Chapter 8: A Fresh Can of Spam</u> before they message me though.

STORY TIME – DISNEY+ HACK

Let's talk about the most significant security breach you have never heard of.

Disney Plus came out in the fall of 2019. They were in direct competition with Netflix, Hulu, Crave, Amazon's Prime TV, and other similar streaming services. One day after their launch, there were 1000 online accounts for sale for as little as $3 each. By the end of the week, there were thousands more for sale.[13]

The media was all over Disney for allowing such a significant lack of security on their site. Disney's reputation would never be restored in the minds of many people.

You are undoubtedly wondering how Disney Plus could have been hacked in its first 24-hours of operation. You are probably shocked that a company like Disney would allow such negligent security on such a huge new service. You are right to wonder.

You might also wonder why we call it "the most significant security breach you have never heard of" if it was all over the news and everyone heard of it. Every news service was talking about how Disney's new streaming service had been hacked.

The problem stemmed from many people making a single mistake that they probably were not even aware of… and hardly any of them were Disney cast members (that's what they call their employees).

---

[13] Disney+ hack
http://footnote13.dbtwl.com

The hacked accounts stem from perhaps the most prevalent single online security risk… using the same passwords on multiple sites. [14] If you recall my search where I found my personal email account had been compromised at least nine times (it was 18 times by the time we went to print). Someone out there has my email address in a list with several passwords that I had used in various sites many years ago.

Now imagine that I signed up for Disney Plus the day it opened on November 12, 2019. Also imagine that I used a password that was on that list. By midnight that first night, someone might have paid up to $20 for my account information, and I didn't even know I was sharing my service.

Typically, these accounts were being sold for under $10 and I heard of some being sold for as little as $3 but that is a significant saving compared to my wife paying $7 every month for the rest of her life (or until Disney raises its prices).

EDIT: Since we started writing this book, a Disney Plus subscription in Canada has gone from $79 per year to $149 per year to maintain premium services.

The benefit would be that you might get a lifetime account for $3 but you might also pay the $3 and find out that my wife changed her password tomorrow. Someone who buys your account login might do something stupid like resetting your password and locking you out, but a quick tech support call and you will be back online and their $3 will have been wasted. Honestly, if you never tried to have four simultaneous logins for your account, you would probably never know that someone else was using it.

This type of hacking is called "credential stuffing" and is, without a doubt, one of the most prevalent security breaches in the world. If your credentials are hacked on one site, meaning someone bad has

---

[14] Disney+ credential stuffing
http://footnote14.dbtwl.com

your email and password combination, and you reuse that email and password arrangement in other places, they are going to find other sites that use them eventually.

Credential Stuffing

A cyberattack where stolen account credentials typically consisting of lists of usernames or email addresses and corresponding passwords are used to gain unauthorized access to user accounts through large-scale automated login requests

---

If you finished the Play Along section in **Chapter 1: Find Your Weakness,** you have already determined if you had any compromised accounts, so you are well ahead of most people. This list is one of the most concise I have seen, but it does not include all breaches so be sure that you are only using each password one time.

We will discuss this further in **Chapter 3: Password-itis.**

Regardless of how many online accounts you have, you really need to concentrate on not allowing yourself to use the same password on multiple sites. If you are going to get hacked, credential stuffing will be the likely method.

This story has two take-aways. First, never believe what you hear or see on the news just because they are an authority. You do not always know their sources. Second, never, never, never use the same password twice. Just don't do it.

TTT – PASSWORD STATS

Welcome to your first Time Travel Tip. Remember that when you see this, you can go to the website **www.DBTWL.com** or **www.DontBeTheWeakestLink.com** and follow for updates on these tips every year. This allows us to keep the content updated so that we don't have to release a new edition of this book as often.

The 2021 **security**.org **pass**word **sur**vey **reve**aled **th**at 68% **of** people **reu**se **t**he **sa**me **pass**word **f**or **mult**iple **sit**es.[15]

Only 12% **of** **peop**le **u**se 12 **o**r **more** **chara**cters **i**n **th**eir **passw**ords. 42% **of** **peop**le **u**se **cur**se **wor**ds. 21% **u**se **th**eir **bir**th **ye**ar, **a**nd 18% **of** **peop**le **u**se **th**eir **pe**t's **na**me **in** **th**eir **passw**ords.

A 2023 **Spyc**loud **repo**rt[16] **mak**es **a cla**im **th**at 72% **of use**rs **we**re **brea**ched **wit**h **a reu**sed AND **previ**ously **expo**sed **pass**word! **Th**at **is** up **fr**om 60% **t**wo **yea**rs **earl**ier.[17]

This **mea**ns **th**at **a pers**on's **acco**unt **in**fo **h**ad **be**en **brea**ched, **a**nd **th**e **brea**ch **deta**ils **we**re **po**sted **o**n **site**s **li**ke **th**e **o**ne **y**ou **te**sted **y**our **em**ail **addr**ess **o**n. **Af**ter **th**e **bre**ach **wa**s **ma**de **pub**lic, **th**ey **st**ill **crea**ted **acco**unts **us**ing **th**e **sa**me **crede**ntials. **We** **ca**n't **b**e **su**re **how many** **we**re **n**ot **awa**re **o**f **th**e **init**ial **bre**ach, **a**nd **how many** **o**f **th**em **ha**ve **a Resp**onse **Ra**nk **o**f 5 **a**nd **ju**st **di**dn't **ca**re.

The 2023 **rep**ort **al**so **fou**nd **th**at 61% **of** **passw**ords **a**re **reu**sed. **If** 61% **of** **passw**ords **a**re **reu**sed **a**nd 72% **of** **hac**ks **inclu**ded **th**ese **passw**ords, **th**at **mea**ns **th**at **ma**ny **o**f **th**e **hac**ks **invo**lved **hac**king **th**e **sa**me **vic**tim **mult**iple **tim**es.

PIN SAFETY

There **is** **a bl**og **po**st **ou**t **the**re **th**at **we**nt **thr**ough 3.4 **mill**ion **discl**osed **PIN**s (**pers**onal **identif**ication **numb**ers) **fr**om **prev**ious **hac**ks **a**nd **th**e **ana**lysis **is chil**ling.[18] **If** **y**ou **a**re **li**ke **m**e **a**nd **lo**ve **numb**ers, **stati**stics, **a**nd **da**ta **analy**tics, **th**en **th**is **po**st **wi**ll **capti**vate **y**ou.

[15] 2021 Security.org Password Survey
http://footnote15.dbtwl.com
[16] 2023 SpyCloud Annual Identity Exposure Report
http://footnote16.dbtwl.com
[17] 2021 SpyCloud Annual Identity Exposure Report
http://footnote17.dbtwl.com
[18] PIN analysis
http://footnote18.dbtwl.com

Not only does it include fascinating facts like 20% of all the PINs in the dataset were 1234, 1111, 0000, and 1212, but it also shows a heatmap analysis that shows a large percentage of people use dates in their PIN.

44% of PINs that end in 84 also start with 19. There are 100 combinations that end in 84. Why would a 1% number be 4400 times higher? Because 1984 is a popular year of birth for PIN holders and a brilliant book. 1985 and 1986 are both way above the numerical average as well. Do not use your birth year as a PIN.

If that doesn't scare you, 50% of all 4-digit PINs appear in the first 426 most popular codes. That means that 4.26% of all PINs make up half of real-world choices.

If you reuse a PIN for credit cards, entry codes, or lock combinations, you clearly do not have a Response Ranking of 1 but if you use a date or something personal, you are probably a 4 or 5. You may want to be a 1 or 2 but if your Knowledge Ranking is a D or F, you simply won't know how insecure it could be to reuse the same PIN everywhere.

SUMMARY

I want to summarize the lessons from this password chapter because passwords are stupid. They are hard to remember, and a dozen people will recommend a dozen different solutions.

You should remember the formula for a great password:

1. Make it long! (15-character minimum)
2. Make it complex! (all four character-types)
3. Use a passphrase
4. Never use the same password more than once!

Try to use spaces unless the site or service doesn't allow them. Don't reset a great password unless you think it has been compromised.

If your work forces you to change your company passwords on a regular schedule, share this book or some of our videos with your boss or the IT team. Our videos are all linked on our website at www.DBTWL.com or on social media. You can search for DBTWL or Shayne Kawalilak on Rumble, TikTok, or YouTube for some videos.

PLAY ALONG

In the chapter 2 play along, we are going to look at your passwords and the password strengths. We will also be looking at default passwords in your life.

Task 2-1 Password Testing

https://www.dbtwl.com/tools

For this task, we will go back to the DBTWL website above or go to www.DBTWL.com and click on Tools. Then scroll down to click the link under "Password Hack Time" and enter some of the passwords that you use to see how quickly they can be hacked.

The site will show various times for each password. I always use the shortest time, assuming the database that holds my credentials has been fully downloaded onto a supercomputer.

Task 2-2 How Common is Your Password?

Stay on the Tools page of the DBTWL website and click on the link under 'Commonly Hacked'. On that page, enter one of your passwords to see how many times it has been compromised.

These compromises aren't necessarily linked to your email address. If you test the password 'Password1!' you will see that it has been compromised over 30,000 times. Obviously more than a few people thought this was a good enough password. These people have a Knowledge Ranking of D or F and probably a Response Ranking of 5.

Task 2-3 Camera Hacking Videos

For this task we are going to watch some videos online of people's TV's and home appliances being hacked. There is no shortage of these videos and you will see that so many people were not even aware that their TVs had cameras.

Go to the www.DBTWL.com site, click on The Book and then Chapter 2 and Cameras.

Task 2-4 Change Your Router Password

www.DBTWL.com/book/chapter2

Go to our website and click on The Book and then Chapter 2 to follow along…

For this task, we are going to change the password of our home router. If you have already changed the password away from the default, congratulations. If not, open the website above for instructions.

Follow the instructions on the site to get to the login screen for the internet router that your ISP gave you when you signed up for their internet service. Somewhere here will be a quick and easy way to change your password. You don't have to do it now, but at least you know how to do it.

Task 2-5 Change a Password

Change any password that you know has been reused. You may have the same password for dozens of websites. Choose one, log into the website, and change your password to something that you have never used before. You will probably have to write this password down until the end of Chapter 3: Password-itis.

_____

_____

_____

_____

_____

_____

_____

_____

_____

_____

_____

_____

_____

_____

_____

_____

_____

_____

_____

_____

CHAPTER 3: PASSWORD-ITIS

You have **undoubtedly heard of** diseases like **appendicitis, bronchitis, hepatitis, and meningitis. I could go** on all day, **but I would like to introduce you to password-itis.** The **only cure for this tech disease is to stop remembering passwords. You heard that correctly. Say it out loud so your ears get the full effect...** "**Stop remembering passwords**".

You **might not be thrilled with me right** now. **I told you how to** find out if **you**'ve been **compromised, and you probably found out** that you were. **I told you to make sure you use great passwords which** are long and **complex. I told you to use passphrases instead of passwords. Then I told you to never use a password more than once.** Now **I am saying not to memorize them.**

But I am going to make you happy because I am going to show you how to securely remember all your passwords with trivial effort and less damage to your brain.

WHAT IS A PASSWORD MANAGER?

A 2021 NordPass study found that most of us use around 100 passwords.[19] It is no wonder why we are having trouble remembering them all and why people make poor decisions here with their security. Some people write each one on a sticky note or in a spreadsheet, some make all the passwords the same, and some have a keyboard system to remember them.

None of these solutions are sufficient today.

STORY TIME – ELLEN

I want to tell you a story that I know you will enjoy more with the help of a video. For that, go to our website at www.DBTWL.com and click on "The Book" link up top and then on Chapter 3 and then Story Time. On that website you can watch a great video from a talk show that should make you reconsider ever writing a password down again.

As I was watching Ellen DeGeneres talk about a fantastic new tool to document all her passwords, she held up a book. The book was called Internet Password Minder.

Ellen started acting stunned, maybe not as stunned as I was, but she clearly saw the irony in labeling the book containing all your private credentials with the words "Internet Password Minder" on the cover. She then pushed the boundaries a bit by suggesting another book, but she also said something that blew my mind. She stated she bought this password tracking book online.

---

[19] NordPass Password Study
http://footnote19.dbtwl.com

Suddenly, I gasped at the possibility that this funny skit could be real.

Could it be possible? Could people be tricked into purchasing a book for tracking passwords? Apparently so. There are dozens of them available online. Most say what they are in bold letters on the cover, just like the one Ellen had on her show.

To make matters worse, it didn't take long for me to realize that my mother and my in-laws both have books for their passwords.

To be clear, it would be more secure to buy a blank notebook for this purpose, and it would save you a lot of money.

These books would each qualify as a password manager, albeit a horrible one. I have seen so many people using dreadful password managers ranging from sticky notes to notes under a keyboard.

ACCEPTABLE WRITING

I will confess that in my presentations, I have been known to tell the audience that I do allow, and encourage, writing down of passwords in a couple instances.

The first instance would be if you were in a position of being responsible for a family member who had issues remembering login information for websites, or was on the way to having memory issues soon. In this case, do what you must do to get this information from the person as quickly as possible.

I have some personal experience with trying to find credentials for loved ones who can't help you any longer. It is a rough task with banking information but with social media companies it can be a nightmare.

Let's discuss the other instance in a few minutes.

For now, we need to understand that a password manager is exactly what it sounds like. It is a system outside of your memory to remember all your passwords. Now that we have covered some of the less encouraged versions, we are going to discuss more secure solutions and why we need them.

You need a password manager that can remember infinite passwords with websites, usernames, and notes, and allows fast and simple recall for each use.

SOME SECURITY MISCONCEPTIONS

Most people treat their home differently from the office and that is a problem for a few reasons, but mostly it is because of flaws in our understanding of the differences between home and work.

1. Companies have password rules.
2. Office passwords are more important.
3. The home is more secure.

None of these truths are as simple as they sound, yet they are things that most of us believe without hesitation.

1. Companies have password rules

Most companies have rules, but the insinuation with the statement is that this enhances security. We already covered that many professional geeks still believe that scheduled changing of passwords is inherently secure. Clearly, not all rules enhance security.

By the end of this book, everyone should be convinced of this truth.

Some companies require that your password be a minimum of eight characters, and we covered how insecure that rule is. I have even heard of a company that banned password managers from being installed on their network.

I would love to speak to the IT Department that came up with this rule because I can't think of a single reason for it. Nor can I imagine a world where a password manager would be less secure than any alternative.

2. Office passwords are more important

Typical companies have layers of security with redundancies in place that make passwords less important in the grand scheme on the basis that they are a single component of a larger security system. But passwords are still required. If the password is the only form of authentication, which it shouldn't be, then the value of what it's protecting should not be significant.

You may think that your personal information is worth less than your company's, but to think that the password to your company's server is more important than the password to your personal banking account or tax account is completely wrong.

You are the only one protecting your personal data and your identity online. That office has a team of professional geeks protecting it.

Banks and companies that you deal with also have teams protecting their data, but I cannot vouch for them because I don't know them. I didn't hire or vet them for that role. I don't even know the data management policies of that company so why would I trust them to protect my data any more than what I am doing? I am responsible for securing my authentication methods the same way I am responsible for protecting the PIN for my bank cards and credit cards.

If you treat your personal data with more regard, you will treat your company data with more regard as well. This is most easily accomplished by educating yourself and moving your Knowledge Ranking closer to the "A".

We should also consider that the office will have redundant backups in order to recover from data loss. What are you doing at home to protect your data? If you lost all your family photos and personal documents, would you be able to recover them from a backup or archive?

As an aside, please make sure that you aren't counting on the redundancy of a service like Google Drive or OneDrive for backups of your data. At the minimum, you should be backing up all your data to a USB device as well. There is a huge difference between redundancy and backups.

Maybe your home is more important than you first thought?

3. The home is more secure

The concept that your home is more secure, because you know the people with access to your home, might have some merit to it. I do have two problems with this line of thinking.

First, the gatekeepers in your office should have training on how to prevent unknown individuals from getting into secure locations. The people in your home do not have this training.

Second, your co-workers are all trusted by the company, but there are many people who might enter your home who are not vetted at all. Take a moment and consider the following people who might enter your home: a gardener, cleaning staff, gas or electric company, contractors, landlords, insurance inspectors, your neighbor, drunken kids your children invited over when you were out of town... the list could go on. Do you not remember the Tom Cruise breakout hit, Risky Business?[20]

The primary motivation for my presentations on this topic has been to make people more secure at home. The fact is, if your security

---

[20] Risky Business
http://footnote20.dbtwl.com

is weak at home, you will form bad habits. Those bad habits will eventually make it into the workplace. The opposite is also true.

> You will more likely be the entry point for a future corporate compromise if you have bad habits with your personal data.

Hopefully, now that you have more tools and information at your disposal, your Knowledge Ranking will move up and farther away from that "F". We do this by not only preventing bad habits from forming, but by developing good habits.

One of those good habits is gaining familiarity with a password manager.

WHY USE A PASSWORD MANAGER?

The reason we should use a password manager is straightforward. Our brains can only hold so much information. Rather than reset passwords when we forget them, or use passwords that are short and easy to remember, or use the same password multiple times, it's much better to set one that's great and document it in a password manager.

A good password manager does not just allow us to recall a vast quantity of password or passphrases, it also allows them to be extremely long and secure, and it stores the website, username, password history, and notes.

There is one additional HUGE reason to use a password manager but we are going to discuss that one in <u>Chapter 11: Hitting Closer to Home</u>. It will be worth the wait.

There are many different password managers, but for this chapter we're going to focus on five options.

1. **KeePass**
2. **Last**pass
3. **Bitwa**rden
4. 1**Password**
5. **Robo**Form

TTT – TOP PASSWORD MANAGERS

On the **www.DBTWL.com** website under **Chap**ter 3 and Time Travel Tips, we will **ende**avor to **publ**ish our **favo**rite **password managers each ye**ar.

As for **public recommen**dations, I **f**ind the Wired reviews easy to under**stand, even though I don't agree with them on all their choices. Here is the**ir 2024 list **o**f top password managers.[21]

SUMMARY OF OPTIONS

I add**ed **KeePass **to the list beca**use I beli**eve it is the only opt**ion in the list that allows for local stor**age of the credential data**base. All the other solutions encrypt the stored credentials and allow them to be stored out on the internet.

KEEPASS

Keep**ass has new options which allow for some cloud altern**atives, but where Keepass really shines is that it allows you to store your passwords in a local file or on a USB key.

The benefit of cloud stor**age is that it is avail**able to you anywhere with a web browser that you can log into your password manager. The downside is that it is also available to anyone on the internet if

---

[21] 2024 Wired Password Manager reviews
http://footnote21.dbtwl.com

they can hack into it. They are secure, but the opportunity exists for a breach simply because of their storage location.

The likelihood of a password manager company losing your data is minimal in my mind (not impossible anymore though). For a highly technical person who understands encryption and security, storing a local database may be a good option. For a standard computer user however, securing that local database will bring about its own security issues and, in my mind, isn't a worthy option.

Even if using the cloud version of KeePass, I found that the interface was not as user-friendly as the alternatives in this list.

Therefore, everything we discuss from here on will be about the four remaining password managers in our list.

Let's get right into Lastpass, the company that actually did let someone steal encrypted user password vaults.

LASTPASS

I will confess that the vast majority of my experience with password managers has been with LastPass and I have stayed with them for over a decade for two main reasons…

First, they grandfathered my old "Enterprise" account so that I could never achieve the same level of features from the other services for the same price.

Second, LastPass has been hacked and compromised on more than one occasion, the last as recently as 2022. You may be thinking that this would be a reason to move away from LastPass, but just being the big boy on the block has made them a huge target for hackers. Even being the largest target, to my knowledge, they have never lost any user data.

Not that data hasn't been lost, because they did lose the entire encrypted vaults of millions of users, but they proved their "zero knowledge" architecture would allow no one access to user data without that one master password. And they proved that they could not lose that master password because they didn't have it.

If you had a great password that met the standards from the last chapter, then you probably have no worries. Don't get me wrong, I did change a few of my passwords, well, more than a few.

This is a company whose job is to secure personal information from the best of the best hackers, and they have been tested.

But it hasn't all been sunshine and roses for LastPass.

They were purchased by another tech company and then that company was purchased again in 2019. I admit, I was a little unnerved back then with all the changes, but apparently my worries were unfounded.

LastPass offers a solid solution for a decent price. They have a free version available, but it has some limitations that may be onerous to some users as you can only access your passwords on a single device.

The structure, usability, and rich feature set is second to none, which made switching to other password managers difficult, though necessary for the research on this book. The paid versions are some of the industry's best deals for both individuals and families.

At the end of the day, I still recommend LastPass because I think it has a great user interface, the best user experience, and a decent price. It also has what I consider to be the best free option available.

Charles believes that the occurrence of too many successful attacks and the allowance of entire user password vaults to be stolen, despite still having top encryption, was a step too far.

I understand his position.

BITWARDEN

Bitwarden has a completely free version which includes a decent list of features. The paid version is only $10 per year and includes a much more robust feature set which allows it to make every reviewer's list. If you need these full features and are on a budget, then this is the lowest cost I've seen.

I have, however, not found Bitwarden to be quite as user-friendly as the other options on this list. This needs to be a consideration if you don't love technology or have issues learning new software and applications.

I have also had issues with credentials not being saved automatically and some glitchy reactions that would require a much cleaner user interface to make the top of my list.

They do tout some new features coming as they are promoting some interesting ideas, like password-less access... time will tell if these features are secure or beneficial.

1PASSWORD

1Password does not offer a free version outside a short trial, but it has the same rich features as other password managers, and it is simple to use. Its paid offerings are in the same realm as LastPass and other solutions but where it really shines is on large family accounts. 1Password is the only solution I have seen which allows you to add individuals to a family account and for only a dollar per month per user, it would become the best family deal before too long.

I believe that 1Password was the first solution to test your passwords against known, compromised, credentials. LastPass does this now as well (with the paid version), and others may be following suit by the time you are reading this. Considering how many credentials we found compromised in chapter one, a feature that warns you before using a password that has already been hacked, is a great offering.

I experienced some sporadic issues with saving passwords for new websites, but they were less frequent than I experienced with BitWarden and the user interface, although not as simply as LastPass, makes it worth the effort.

1Password is the highest individual and family pricing.

ROBOFORM

Until recently, I had never heard of RoboForm. I have tested it with some basic tests and have been thoroughly impressed. It has all the features that you would need in a password manager with a very intuitive interface.

I was expecting RoboForm to have more bugs because it is so new. Its full feature product has only been on the market with the free version since 2017. I haven't really run through more than basic usages but found less bugs than more established competitors.

As far as pricing, it is in the middle of the field for both individual and family pricing.

Where you may find large discounts is for corporate pricing. I have personal experience with using RoboForm for a large non-profit and the discounts they gave us were not even in the ballpark of the more expensive options in this list. They were substantially less expensive for a comparable product.

PRICING TABLE

	Free Option	Monthly Individual	Annual Individual	Monthly Family	Annual Family
Lastpass	Full	$ 2.13	$ 25.56	$ 2.75	$ 33.00
BitWarden	Full	$ 1.20	$ 14.40	$ 4.50	$ 54.00
1Password	14-day	$ 3.75	$ 45.00	$ 5.99	$ 72.00
RoboForm	Full	$ 2.33	$ 27.96	$ 4.02	$ 49.00

All prices in Canadian Dollars

While these prices fluctuate often, without corporate plans and volume discounts, the best deal you will probably find on these products will be around US Thanksgiving.

WHY NOT USE A BROWSER?

A question that I hear frequently at my presentations is, 'why not just use a browser to store your passwords?' and the answer could be as simple as, Shayne said never use a browser to store passwords.

If that is not enough, then Charles agrees, and that should hopefully be enough.

If you still need convincing, let's look at some downsides to a browser remembering passwords. Do you trust the person who owns that browser to never share or release this private information, either deliberately or by accident?

Keep in mind that their first order of business, their primary function of existing for most of them, is to collect as much of your information as they can gather and sell it to whoever will pay for it. Their second priority is connecting your search engine results to you as promptly as possible.

By reviewing your browser settings, you will discover that numerous security features are turned off by default. Wouldn't you rather trust a company who has your private data security as one of their top goals?

Charles brings up another concern with a compromised website having the ability to read these browser-stored credentials at some point? We haven't heard of such a vulnerability yet, but the fact is, that if the tool that you use to open websites is the same tool that you use to store your passwords, it is possible that one may be used to attack the other without you knowing.

Task 3-1 Install a Password Manager

www.DBTWL.com/book/chapter3

The links will exist on our website at www.DBTWL.com then click on The Book and then Chapter 3

The Play Along portion of this chapter will be quite simple... choose a password manager and install it. Log into three sites you use often, like your bank, email, or gaming sites, and watch how it remembers your credentials. The links to the most recent list of password managers will be on the site along with their respective websites which you can find on www.DBTWL.com under Book and Chapter 3.

www.lastpass.com

www.bitwarden.com

www.1password.com

www.roboform.com

Task 3-2 Store a Password

Go back to previous chapters and connect to some websites that you have set passwords for and log into them. Your new password manager should offer to store the passwords automatically. It should also prompt you if you try to save a site with a password that has already been used.

Task 3-3 Confirm No Duplicate Passwords

In the Chapter 2 Play Along section, you changed passwords of compromised sites, but did you make sure that those passwords had not been used before?

Go back to Play Along task 1-1 in Chapter 1: Find Your Weakness and change any passwords that have been used more than once so that every password is unique and has never been duplicated anywhere with your email address or username.

Don't forget to make sure that you are using spaces and passphrases wherever possible.

_____

CHAPTER 4: JOIN THE SEARCH

In the 1990s everyone was trying to get onto the information superhighway. Then we all talked about the World Wide Web and the Net. Then it was all about the internet and now we get online, on the web, or straight to the cloud.

Whatever words you use to describe your online journey, the next two chapters are all about the on-ramps and off-ramps; the tools and services that we use to get our eyeballs in front of that information.

Many people confuse a web browser with a search engine and vice versa. Alphabet (the company), owns a browser called Chrome and a search engine called Google. Informed people with a Response Rank of 1 or 2, will probably rarely use either. You can use Edge or Brave (different browsers) but your search engine can still be Google.

Microsoft owns the browser called Edge and the Bing search engine. It is confusing, but the two popular companies line up like this:

- Company: **Microsoft**
  - o Browser: **Edge**
  - o Search Engine: **Bing**
- Company: **Alphabet**
  - o Browser: **Chrome**
  - o Search Engine: **Google**

SEARCH ENGINES

> "Search engines today are the epitome of confirmation bias."
> ~ Neil deGrasse Tyson

What does Neil mean by that statement? He is talking about how search engines track who you are and feed you results that you would be more interested in reading and viewing!

When I install a new computer or set up a new user profile, I always install three or four web browsers. I often set something other than Edge as the default browser, and I usually change their default search engine for all browsers depending on their needs.

A search engine is an application or tool that allows you to search through collections of information about anything on the internet.

When I was starting out in IT, the most popular search engines were AOL, Yahoo, Lycos, Excite, Altavista, WebCrawler, etc. Unless you are over 40, you have probably never heard of most of these companies. You have undoubtedly heard of Google though. Google came into the market with a unique approach.

They wanted to sell advertising space on search pages and collect billions of pieces of information about the people who were searching and what they were searching for. They now have trillions of pieces of this valuable data, and Google is one of the largest companies in the world and without a doubt, the most influential.

The search engine is a tool that is difficult to rate and recommend simply because different search engines have different functionalities and limitations. If ads really bother you, then you might have to steer clear of a search engine that is perfect for another person. Here are some of the key components of various search engines:

- Results that match your query
- A simple interface
- Search options
- Filtering and fine-tuning with search suggestions
- Unobtrusive ads
- Dated results
- Privacy of your searches

The perfect search engine for you will probably depend on what aspects you find important from the list above.

Microsoft's Bing search engine put up a noble effort to dethrone Google but unless something drastic happens, they simply do not have what it takes to grab the #1 spot. They are a noticeable #2 in the world because, with over 90% of the world's searches, Google Search is the current reigning champ by a colossal margin.[22]

EDIT: With every edit of this book, I have to change my opinion of Bing as a search engine. 2023 marked a significant shift as Bing invested a billion dollars to become the first major search engine to successfully implement AI. Initially, the results were nothing short of amazing. I could see a time when they could impact Google's usage (which makes me sound crazy to some).

---

[22] Search Engines
http://footnote22.dbtwl.com

I used to use **Dogpile** because it returned the top **Google** responses, as well as the top responses from several other search engines. In the last fifteen years it has gotten way too ad-intensive, as have many search engines, and it currently mainly relies on search results from Bing and Google. I can search both those sites by myself without having to deal with all the ads.

The amount of information you freely give away by searching should shock you. This information can be used to market items to you that will simply wear you down over time and suddenly you are purchasing items you didn't need. These companies are perfecting the online version of impulse buying.

TTT – TOP SEARCH ENGINES

Currently, these are the most used search engines in the world (as of January 2024):

1. **Google** 92.94%
2. **Bing** 2.86%
3. **Yahoo** 1.85%
4. **Baidu** (**China**) 1.37%
5. **Yandex** (**Russia**) 1.1%
6. **DuckDuckGo** 0.67%

When I started talking about search engines, I mentioned I change all browser applications to the same default search engine, and it's only fitting that I tell you what I use and why. Since this book is about online privacy, you might be able to guess why I am talking about search engines so much.

I will tell you that at the current time, I use **DuckDuckGo** as a search engine on almost all my browsers except **Brave** (where I use the **Brave** search engine). I have tested it several times with various searches, and the discrepancies I have seen between results are not significant and sometimes the difference is preferred.

Charles and I have discussed this in depth, and we believe DuckDuckGo is the obvious choice for a private search engine today and almost everyone should use it.

The two reasons that I use DuckDuckGo are that it does not track any of your searches and it is an open search engine because it doesn't have algorithms directing your searches to the things that they want you to see. The creators designed it to guide you transparently to the results you were searching for.

With this in mind, I have to tell you that my relationship with DuckDuckGo has not all been pleasant. In May 2022, security researcher Zack Edwards, revealed that DuckDuckGo was allowing some tracking from both bing.com and linkedin.com because of an existing contract with Microsoft. It was minimal tracking, and they shared no personal info about you (because they don't know it).[23]

In 2019, Rich Granville accused DuckDuckGo of having at least two tracking cookies in their search engine, and I couldn't find any response to the claim from DuckDuckGo.[24]

DuckDuckGo went into 2022 as the "privacy browser", but in March of that year they opted for a different approach by limiting some media outlets in its search results. It is prioritizing media outlets based on what some corporate fact checker believes is more accurate. So much for getting rid of the gatekeepers and allowing people to use their judgments to determine what is accurate and good reporting. Many of their fans have expressed disdain for this move.[25]

I will point out that if history is any judge, the person pointing at someone and yelling propaganda is typically the person spreading

---

[23] DuckDuckGo and Microsoft
http://footnote23.dbtwl.com
[24] DuckDuckGo tracking cookies
http://footnote24.dbtwl.com
[25] DuckDuckGo censorship comments
http://footnote25.dbtwl.com

the **propaganda**, so it is more **likely** that **DuckD**uckGo is **promo**ting **misinfo**rmation with **their news feed** than **preven**ting it. This doesn't **affect me** so much **as I don't** use **DuckD**uckGo **to search for news…** any **more**.

We **ha**ve **NOT foun**d a **comp**any **resp**onse as to why **they foun**d **the**se **betra**yals of **their fundam**ental **values acce**pt**able** or **neces**sary.[26] And it may be **some**how, that **they don't even see them** as **betra**yals.

Charles **hat**es **endor**sing **any**thing **specific beca**use **corpor**ations **change their pos**ition **or get caught ly**ing **so often** that he doesn't **want** to be **caught** up in **their fail**ures. He **sounds** so much **smar**ter than me, but **that's partly my self-deprec**ating **writing sty**le.

I **ke**ep **us**ing **DuckD**uckGo **for many writing** and **work-rela**ted **searches, but when look**ing **for news** or **information about curr**ent **events, I u**se **different search eng**ines. Since I **change the**se **daily** and I **often commit the same search** on **mult**iple **search engines, I won't promo**te **any**one in **particular.**

Look back at the Neil deGrasse **Tys**on **quo**te a **few pag**es back. If you **only ever search for news about sport**ing **events, you will get a lot more news about sport**ing **events even when you're** not **look**ing **for it**.

Brave **is un**i**que in** that **both the brow**ser and **search eng**ine **are called Bra**ve.

EDIT: They were **uni**que **but now DuckD**uckGo has **a brow**ser and a **search eng**ine with **the same name as we**ll.

Please **sign up for our mail**ing **list** on **www.DB**TWL.com or **www.DontBeThe**Weakestlink.com **and get notified when we upda**te

---

[26] DuckDuckGo censorship decisions
http://footnote26.dbtwl.com

readers on browser and search engine options and features as companies implement changes.

REVENUE STREAMS

You should consider one additional thing before assessing how safe your personal information is with Google, or any browser or search engine that relies on ad revenue and selling your personal information to advertisers.

With no technical knowledge, just relying on common sense, how smart is it to believe that a company that makes money collecting, trading, and selling your personal data will provide a private browsing experience?

This is the primary function of Chrome and Edge. Browsers remain free mostly because, to companies like Alphabet and Microsoft, the revenue they bring in with search engines, ad revenue, and selling personal data, would make any operational costs insignificant.

> If you are getting a service or product for free, then YOU AND YOUR DATA are the service or product in the transaction.

Those two tech giants are not alone as advertising revenue is now Amazon's number one profit stream ahead of sales and web hosting with AWS. Amazon makes more profit from selling advertisements for the things it sells than it makes from the actual things that it sells.[27]

---

[27] Amazon Ad Revenue
http://footnote27.dbtwl.com

Other browsers don't have colossal parent companies propping them up, so they need to show a profit. Firefox does this primarily by selling its hundreds of millions of user eyeballs to a search engine (currently Google). Their ad revenue from 2021 was just under $60M.[28]

Brave makes its money by selling ad space. They strip ads from websites and replace them with their own ads. This saves the time of downloading the sites' ads, making your browsing slightly faster. It also sends advertisements to your desktop that are not aimed at you personally through profile manipulation. Brave doesn't care who you are, everyone gets the same ad.

This has been a contentious act. If we sold an advertiser space on the **DBTWL** website, anyone who visited our website on a Brave browser would see another company's advertisement. As Brave gains market share, this may disrupt the ad game online but they aren't there yet.

Search engines have their own ads in the search results you see. Search engines label their own ads in the search results with a small "sponsored" or something obscure that they hope you will miss and click on their advertiser instead of the search results you were looking for.

When I see DuckDuckGo or Brave post ads in my browser, I know they are making money off my clicks. Charles and I don't mind clicking ads occasionally to ensure that these companies can keep the lights on. I will never click an advertisement on Google. More about that later.

Google makes $20B a year collecting money from advertisers because it has the largest public database with which to target

---

[28] Firefox Ad Revenue
http://footnote28.dbtwl.com

specific users. It is hard to believe that my privacy has any interest to them.

> My desire for privacy is in direct conflict with Google's primary source of income.

How do we protect our personal information in a world where companies like Google and Facebook are making billions of dollars a month collecting every piece of data they can find? What can we do to protect ourselves?

First off, I think it is important to understand that if you have a Knowledge Ranking of A or B, and a 1 or 2 on the Response Ranking, you probably already avoid Alphabet (which is Google, Chrome, Android, Gmail, YouTube, etc.)[29], Meta (Facebook, WhatsApp, and Instagram)[30], Microsoft (Edge, Bing, LinkedIn, etc.)[31], and Apple[32]. There is simply no way for you to compete with their desire to use your information to sell something to you or others like you.

Where you need to use them, you lock them out of your personal information as much as possible.

I use these companies despite them all having been caught lying to the public about protecting their data and the footnotes are just examples. There are worse things they do with your data and have been doing for an extended period of time.[33] Feel free to search for more examples on your own. These companies have shown little

---

[29] Google Privacy
http://footnote29.dbtwl.com
[30] Facebook Privacy
http://footnote30.dbtwl.com
[31] Microsoft Privacy
http://footnote31.dbtwl.com
[32] Apple Privacy
http://footnote32.dbtwl.com
[33] Government and Big Tech Privacy Concerns
http://footnote33.dbtwl.com

regard for user privacy and you need to weigh your personal privacy against your desire to be online.

I currently own only one tablet from Apple for my daughter's art. Charles does not use Chrome (except at work), Gmail, or Facebook, but uses YouTube (until he finds a reliable alternative at least). Solutions from BitChute, **Rumble**, and Gab TV are coming close. You can see by our online habits, which one of us is more concerned about the privacy of our data.

Keep in mind that I do jump through a lot of hoops to ensure that these companies aren't getting my approval for anything that they don't need, for my usability of their platform and services. I also understand that this does not mean that they are acting in accordance with the agreements that I click on.

Charles is not a big fan of hoop-jumping.

PART OF THE PROBLEM

On multiple occasions I have seen both Google and Facebook promoting criminal activity as part of their standard advertising practices.

If they ever try to hide it, I have many screenshots of the actual evidence that a Google search provided advertisements above search results, where those advertised links are taking victims to sites that will either infect their computers or capture data illegally.

In one instance that I complained to Facebook about, they were promoting a discounted rail ticket that looked like a great deal. I was actually very interested but when I clicked on the link (there were not many red flags), my browser and security applications lost their minds. I instantly received half a dozen warnings that this site was trying to steal and track and install stuff.

I was shocked. How did I get duped?

And then I was upset with Facebook. I had assumed that they vetted their advertisers. Nope. It turns out that anyone could post an advertisement as anyone they wanted with little quality control, if any.

I considered spending a few thousand dollars to place a Google advertisement telling people about this great security feature but then when people opened the ad site it would change the default search engine to all browsers to Duck Duck Go.

On google I could set up an ad that would prevent people from loading Facebook by having people to allow me to change a file on their computer.

But then I couldn't get over that I would be the bad guy, doing the bad things, to peoples' computers without their permission. But it was fun to think about it for a while.

THE DECEPTION OF AI

I am sure that you have heard about all the Artificial Intelligence (AI) tools available recently. The issue I have is that most people hear "AI" and think Skynet from the Terminator movies, and that is not quite what we are dealing with. Current AI is closer to a clever search engine than Skynet.

My largest issue currently is that because these AI models are all programmed by humans, and nowhere near self-learning computers from science fiction movies and books, they suffer from that programming.

Microsoft implemented ChatGPT4 into the Bing search engine before anyone else and the results were amazing. So amazing that my Microsoft Edge usage jumped from 10% to 25% almost overnight. The AI engine appears to have gotten stupider in the next six months, but it still surpasses most other search engines.

Google has tried to implement their own AI on two occasions. Each instance was a disaster. In 2023, Google implemented their Bard AI, but it didn't take long for someone to post evidence of Bard outright lying about simple searchable facts.

Alphabet, Google's parent company, lost over $100 billion in valuation that week. [34]

In February 2024 Google took another kick at the can. They released Google Gemini, which turned out to be a controversial AI graphics model. In researching links for this event, I found multiple descriptions that claim the AI had "alleged bias". [35]

This is wholly inaccurate reporting, and a vast number of people criticized the AI model as being filled with bigoted programming and described it as a racist and sexist tool. [36]

Alphabet (Google) lost another $90 billion that week. [37]

Google apologized almost instantly when the internet became flooded with screenshots of the AI interactions. Gemini showed that Elon Musk might not have been far from the truth when he tweeted that Gemini's image generation feature exposed Google and "made their insane racist, anti-civilizational programming clear to all." [38]

CANVAS FINGERPRINTING

Before we get to this chapter's amazing story time, I want to know if you have ever heard of 'canvas fingerprinting'?

---

[34] Google Bard AI
http://footnote34.dbtwl.com
[35] Google's alleged bias
http://footnote35.dbtwl.com
[36] Google Gemini AI
http://footnote36.dbtwl.com
[37] Alphabet stock depreciation
http://footnote37.dbtwl.com
[38] Elon Musk: Not a fan of Gemini
http://footnote38.dbtwl.com

This is a system that tech and online marketing companies use to identify you. Sometimes you aren't logged into your account but Google, Amazon, Microsoft, Facebook… and many others, still want to know who you are.

These companies track hundreds of data points about your computer from your operating system, browsers you have installed (not necessarily the one you are using), your processor, Ram, and hard drive properties, your version of Acrobat Reader and a list of the fonts that you have installed. They track virtually anything that is trackable to build a fingerprint for your computer that can be more significant to identifying you than your login information to marketing companies.

I will show you an example using your computer fingerprint in the Play Along section in a few pages.

STORY TIME – TARGET ADVERTISING

~ from NYT article (February 19, 2012) by Charles Duhigg (full article available on our website at www.DBTWL.com or www.DontBeTheWeakestLink.com)

A man walked into a Target outside Minneapolis and demanded to see the manager. He was clutching coupons that had been sent to his daughter, and he was furious, according to an employee who took part in the conversation.

"My daughter got this in the mail!" he said. "She's still in high school, and you're sending her coupons for baby clothes and cribs? Are you trying to encourage her to get pregnant?"

The manager didn't have any idea what the man was talking about. He looked at the mailer. Sure enough, it was addressed to the man's daughter and contained advertisements for maternity clothing, nursery furniture, and pictures of smiling infants. The manager apologized and agreed to look into it.

The manager called the father a few days later to apologize again.

On the phone, the father was somewhat abashed. "I had a talk with my daughter," he said. "It turns out there's been some activities in my house I haven't been completely aware of. She's due in August. I owe you an apology."[39]

There is a significant amount of data being taken from people that they simply do not know is being captured.

The revenue streams for these companies are not restricted to data collections through browsers, search engines, or other easily visible methods. The story above with Target, showed that large companies are reviewing purchase patterns with chilling results.

Don't go hating on Target either. They are not the only retailer with a 'predictive analytics' department, they just have one of the best. It started with store loyalty cards and has exploded. Not only do the stores know who you are and what you usually purchase, but they make a habit of tracking how far you drive to your local store, how often you shop at other locations, how many coupons you use, which credit cards you have made purchases with, and much more.

And if they think you are worth the investment, they can purchase more information from many sources selling everything from your educational and work history to your income and travel habits.

Target has spent decades learning our buying habits and the article states that Target was "able to identify about 25 products that, when analyzed together, allowed (them) to assign each shopper a 'pregnancy prediction' score. More important, (they) could also estimate her due date to within a small window, so Target could send coupons timed to specific stages of her pregnancy."

---

[39] Target Targeted Ads
http://footnote39.dbtwl.com

If you enjoy the data science as much as I do, I would encourage you to read the whole article. It goes into detail of how they have looked for patterns and how shoppers form habits.

How can we all move our Knowledge Ranking closer to an A and use that knowledge to affect our Response Ranking?

PLAY ALONG

In this chapter's Play Along section, we are going to see if we can prove that your searches affect your profile for these large tech companies.

We also have a surprise for those of you with Gmail accounts. Let's dig into the homework for Chapter 4: Join the Search.

Task 4-1 Google Searches

www.google.com

The first thing we are going to do is open a web browser to www.google.com and then search for the following word, "cuttlefish". When the results come up, click on one link, go back to the search results, click on a different link, go back to the search and click on a third link.

Now do a Google search for "mermaid wedding dress" and click on three links there as well.

Do the same thing for "From Misery to Happiness poetry book" and click on three unrelated links.

If you have recently searched for one of these exact items, swap it out with my name "Shayne Kawalilak". If you have recently searched for me, then we might have other issues to discuss.

You won't notice the effects of this task immediately, but over the next week, be aware of the ads that you see when you are going about your daily tasks.

If you want to see images of these tasks to help you complete them, please go to our website and click on Book > Chapter 4 > Play Along.

Task 4-2 Amazon Searches

www.amazon.com

Open your browser and go to your local Amazon webpage but do not log into your Amazon account (amazon.com, amazon.ca, amazon.au, amazon.co.uk, etc.) or log out if you are already logged in.

Now search for the same three items you just searched for on Google. If this is "Cuttlefish", "mermaid wedding dress", and "From Misery to Happiness poetry book", then go through and click on a couple of items for each of these searches.

Once again, even though you were not logged into your Amazon account, when you log into your Amazon account again, you will probably see ads for these items that Amazon should not have expected that you would be interested in.

Task 4-3 Set Default Search Engine

Open your favorite web browser, whether it be Chrome, Edge, or whatever. Now click on the three dots in the top right corner and select Settings.

On the left menu or use the search feature, click on "Search engine" and pull down the choice to change your default search engine to DuckDuckGo.

Task 4-4 Look at Your Fingerprint

Let's go back to the www.DBTWL.com website and click on The Book > Tools > then Canvas Fingerprinting.

This will take you to a site where you can go through your fingerprint assessment to see what your browser is allowing companies to take without asking.

Task 4-5 www.gmail.com

This is a bonus for this chapter if you have a Gmail account. If you do not have one, do not create one. Consider yourself blessed and be an observer for the next few minutes. I will try to remember to put screenshots on the website under The Book > Chapter 4 > Play Along.

For those of you who have a Gmail account, go to Gmail (or Google or YouTube) and log into your account in the top right.

Before you move any further, take a moment to sit back and close your eyes. Concentrate hard on what personal information you have given Alphabet. Think about what Google, Gmail, YouTube, Chrome, or Android have been directly told by you. Keep that information in mind when you continue.

a. Log into your Gmail account
b. Click on your picture in the top right corner
c. Click on "Manage your Google Account"
d. Click on "Data & Privacy"
e. Scroll down to "Personalized Ads"
f. Click on "My Ad Center"

Do they know your education level, your age, how much money you make, whether you are married? If they had anything blatantly wrong, let us know via our website or social media.

They knew me quite well except for a few items. I don't know how they evaluate income but seeing that there are only three categories and I live in a world with billionaires, I don't think I fit in the high-income category.

My 17-year-old son, who is basically unemployed, is apparently in the "moderately high income" and works for a "very large employer".

Scroll through the categories. Click and read about where this information is being used. Change anything that you would like. This is one rare place where you get to tell Google they are wrong, and they will listen… even if they weren't wrong.

_____

_____

_____

_____

_____

_____

_____

_____

_____

_____

_____

_____

_____

_____

_____

_____

_____

_____

CHAPTER 5: THE INFORMATION SUPERHIGHWAY

In the last chapter, we talked about the difference between a browser and a search engine, and we did some digging into how search engines work. I will bet you are still confused though.

With all our talk about search engines in the last chapter, it's time to dig into the browsers, that we use to travel to all these websites.

STORY TIME – THE EU VS. MICROSOFT

In 1997, the European Union (EU) charged Microsoft with willfully sabotaging competition by preventing the old Internet Explorer web browser from being uninstalled from Windows. Microsoft argued the browser was an integral part of the Windows operating system and could not be removed.

They had lied, of course, and the result was a large fine to Microsoft. In 2004, the EU slapped Microsoft with another fine, the largest to date, totaling USD $611M.

Over the next 12 months, Microsoft settled lawsuits with at least four competitors for nearly USD $3B. That is three Billion dollars… with a "B". To top that off, the 2004 EU decision wasn't settled for a while and the EU added subsequent fines for failing to comply with the first order. The total in 2008 was north of USD $2.5B dollars.[40]

The public humiliation and bad press was probably not worth the effort. I don't know anyone who has ever tried uninstalling the Internet Explorer (IE) browser. They simply install an alternate browser to use when accessing the internet.

The browser is the application that you use to look at websites on the internet. So many things you do online, from checking the weather or email, to watching videos, require a web browser on your computer. As a general rule, if you see an address bar on the top of your screen with a "www" or an "http" address, then you are looking at a browser.

BROWSERS

Before we get too deep into browsers, we should discuss the differences between a private browser session, a private browser, and a private search engine.

That hurt me, hopefully it is less confusing in the next few minutes.

---

[40] EU Fines Microsoft
http://footnote40.dbtwl.com

Private Browser Sessions

These are private viewing windows inside your browser that claim browsing data for that window will not be tracked. It should state that the browsing data will not be tracked in the same way as a normal browser window. While there is clearly a privacy benefit to using a private browser window (incognito in Chrome or InPrivate in Edge), the tracking is not turned off during the browsing session. Once the session is closed, it simply deletes it. Most of it at any rate.

Private Search Engines

The only two search engines that Charles and I consider to be private search engines are **DuckDuckGo** and **Brave** and we discussed why in the last chapter. To keep things simple, the only two private browsers that we will be discussing will also be **DuckDuckGo** and **Brave**.

I know that the paragraph about them having the same name was going to come back to haunt me.

When searching in **DuckDuckGo**, the information that tracks you simply isn't created, or isn't supposed to be according to the company policies. **DuckDuckGo** can't share your personal information because it doesn't track it while you are browsing. They don't store your search history, so there is nothing to sell to advertisers.

I don't mind the customized ads, but clearly these companies are spending a significant amount of time to determine my habits and sell that data to anyone who would pay for it (directly or indirectly). This is a huge financial resource for many companies in the world of social media, online shopping, browsers, and search engines.

Private Browsers

Today the popular browsers are more varied than they ever have been, but for different reasons. When it was released, Chrome offered more simplicity than Firefox and more functionality than Internet Explorer and it was faster than both of them. But Chrome was, and still is, probably one of the least private ways to surf the internet.

Chrome offers a private browsing mode called "incognito mode" where it saves and stores less data on your computer. The browser has been called out several times for tracking users and allowing extensions to take information from cookies of other websites and to even take user data from the browser itself.

Cookie: Browser Cookie

A small text file stored on your device (computer, mobile, or tablet) by a web browser while you visit a website.

There are so many stories that it is difficult to choose a single footnote but there was a recent story about Microsoft's Edge browser stealing user data from Google's Chrome browser.[41]

Most browsers have some sort of privacy mode available and if you are more than a little curious, you can go online and search for your favorite browser and the words "private browsing" to see what your options are.

Typically, if you click on the top right menu in your browser, you will see private browsing options right near the top.

Privacy has always been important in browsers, but historically, privacy always came behind data farming, speed, and performance. When Brave released their privacy-centric browser in 2019, they changed the game. The browser engine (the code that it was built on)

---

[41] Edge and Chrome
http://footnote41.dbtwl.com

was no faster than Chrome, but the Brave browser was noticeably faster because it didn't download all the advertising and tracking data from websites.

Downloading less 'stuff' means that the browser can load the website faster. It would be similar to using a browser with an ad-blocker extension except those extensions would still allow all the tracking data.

Before the release of the Brave browser, Firefox was the only popular browser that offered any hope of protecting your privacy. You needed to be a professional geek to figure out how to set the browser up to meet this goal. Today, the Brave browser offers all these options (plus some) by default.

Most browsers are not competing on just speed today, but more often they are offering their own ways of showing you they care about your privacy. This is the new metric for grading the "best" browsers and you need to be careful about what you listen to.

There is a myriad of different browsers, and they often serve different needs. You are probably familiar with some of the most popular ones like Edge (the new Internet Explorer), Chrome, or Safari. You can go online to see what the most popular browsers are today, but at the time of writing, the browser wars broke down something like this...

TTT – BROWSER WARS

- **Chrome** 67%
- **Safari** 18%
- **Edge** 5%
- **Firefox** 3%

Statcounter.com has a great user interface which allows you to change the statistics that you see, allowing you to see browser usage on all devices, mobile devices, or desktop computers.[42]

Microsoft includes Edge for free with every installation of the Windows operating system, which makes it popular by default. Google created the Chrome browser in 2008, and it immediately took off, not just because Google promoted it so well, but because Microsoft had gotten lazy and not improved Internet Explorer (the old Edge) since they surpassed Netscape. Internet Explorer eventually put Netscape out of business in 2008 (though they had a single digit market share as early as 2002).

On the website, you will find more current opinions and updates on the browser options. We hope that this makes this book relevant farther into the future than most other technology publications.

TTT – AUTHOR BROWSER USAGE

Currently, I am using the following mixture of browsers…

- **Brave** 50%
- **DuckDuckGo** 15%
- **Opera** 15%
- **Firefox** 15%
- **Edge** 4% (**only for work**)
- **Chrome** 1% (**work mostly**)

Charles, my favorite number 2, thinks he is closer to this usage…

- **Firefox** 75% (99% of personal usage)
- **Chrome** 15% (work only)
- **Edge** 10% (work only)

---

[42] Browser Market Shares
http://footnote42.dbtwl.com

The **Brave** browser was relatively new when we started writing this book, but it has turned out to be quite privacy-centric. **Charles** and **I** both played with it, but **I** had a greater opportunity to work with it than **Charles**. Our usage is still quite low, and until you check out the **TTT**'s from the box above, you will never know where we ended up for our browser usage.

I was using **Brave** much more often when we first set our percentages (they have changed at least three times over this book's creation). **Firefox** announced that they now prevented websites from accessing data in the cookies saved from other websites. This was a big deal for me, so I started using **Firefox** again to test it and some of my browsing has stayed there.

DuckDuckGo now has a browser which is only released for **Android** and **Apple** devices but that will probably change soon and my **Windows** laptop will have a new toy to play with.

EDIT: Since the **DuckDuckGo** browser has been released for **Windows**, I have been using it for specific sites and have been enjoying it. The features are not as robust as **Brave** and there are a couple security features that I would like to see in it, but it is lightweight which is great if you want to leave tabs open for a long time or if you need to install it on older or slower computers or mobile devices.

There is one fashionable offering that comes with all browsers that you **NEVER** want to take advantage of… at least not without serious consideration.

SAVING CREDENTIALS

All browsers offer to save your passwords. Simply saying no is not enough. You should always go into the browser settings and turn off the ability for the browser to remember website credentials and tell it to never ask you again and never to autofill any information, not even your name or address.

If you allow your browser to autofill your contact information to save you time, you will eventually pass that information to websites with invisible forms. The browser might pass on all your personal information without asking for your approval or even making you aware of that data flow.

To promptly find a set of instructions, use your favorite search engine and search for your browser name and the words "disable password" and "disable autofill" as each browser has a unique system to access these settings.

If you need a reason to do this, would it be enough that Charles and I both agree 100% to never save or autofill anything in a browser? We do not hesitate. We simply agree. How often has that happened?

That isn't enough for you?

Do you trust everyone who has access to your computer, laptop, or phone? Do you trust them with all your information? I know you think you are off the hook here because the only people with access to your computer are family members.

So, you leave it unlocked and your five-year-old grandchild, niece/nephew, best friend's kid, etc., sees your unlocked computer and a couple minutes later they are just clicking the mouse... slapping the keyboard... websites are opening... passwords are being automatically filled in... and your bank balance is suddenly being transferred to the first person in your contact list.

I realize that this is an unlikely scenario, but is it possible?

How about the fact that it is a gift for a hacker? If someone ever hacked into your computer, they have ready access to your browser history, so they know what websites you frequent. Using this list, they would simply need to re-open these sites and your browser will log into them for you... or for them.

This will include everything from social media to banking sites. Who doesn't know someone who had a social media account hacked? This is one method they use.

If this seems unlikely too, what will happen if someone steals your computer or laptop? This happens thousands of times a day. Once someone has access to your laptop, it is challenging to prevent them from stealing anything that you have on the device. There are ways to prevent this, but typically they are only used in corporate environments or newer devices.

Charles and I assume that, unless we take extraordinary measures, someone will compromise the data from any stolen device. This is one reason we often limit the amount of data that we store locally on the device. This goes for what we store in browsers that invade your privacy as part of their business practice.

If you still need convincing, then you might be reading the wrong book. You might also change your home page on your browser to www.DontBeTheWeakestLink.com or even to www.DBTWL.com if you are lazy like me.

COOKIES

I am going to tell you about a browser we haven't mentioned yet. I have used many browsers, but none are as private and secure as the Tor browser. It is as convoluted as Firefox used to be and is not something that I would recommend to the average user.

If you want to learn more about what a Tor browser is and when you should use it, I would recommend that you read the Kevin Mitnick book in the Additional Reading List at the end of this book.

One of the nice things that the Tor browser does is it deletes cookies automatically. It is possible to lock down other browsers. My Firefox is quite rigid and often poses issues when I am browsing, which is why I do some work on less secured browsers. Netflix won't run on my Brave browser either.

What do you mean I lost you at cookies? Of course, we aren't talking about the cookies that the dark side promised… and lied about.

That was a Star Wars reference. Sorry if you didn't get it. You might have to just trust me here when I say it was quite funny.

Let's get back to discussing what these cookies are. Think of the Hansel and Gretel story where they left crumbs in the forest to find their way home. Cookies are much the same in that they store all the information about sites that you visit on your computer. The cookies will tell the browser when you last visited, your login information, what items you were looking at, and even the contents of your shopping cart without you logging into a website.

The cookies also tell your browser what preferences you set from regional and language settings to color schemes. All that personalized content comes at a price though, because every single piece of data that you store in a cookie is a piece of data that you make available to hackers, other companies, and the browser you are using. Cookies are often in a simple text file. With some browsers, you make that information available to all the other websites that you visit as well.

In 2022, Firefox released a version update to their browser so different sites could no longer access cookies from one another and in 2023 the Firefox browser enabled "Total Cookie Protection" by default to more users worldwide.[43]

Now that you are good and worried about cookies, let me tell you why you probably don't want to delete them all or terminate your ability to save them on your browsers.

---

[43] Firefox TCP
http://footnote43.dbtwl.com

Not only are cookies extremely convenient, but some of them are necessary for specific sites. Disable all your cookies and see how long it takes for you to get to a website that simply won't function. That would be a significant inconvenience for most of us. It is important to understand what privacy you are putting at risk, and what data you are sharing for the convenience of viewing the websites you visit.

Cookies are inherent security concerns for many reasons.

When a website pops up and asks you if the site can have access to your location, I want you to pause and think about it. Why on earth does Home Depot need to know where your computer or phone is located? To allow you to see regional flyers and sales? To automatically set your "home store" to the one in your neighborhood instead of one on the other side of the country? Are these questions worth trading your GPS location to Home Depot?

Your answer will totally depend on your Response Ranking but with Charles a 2, and me being a 4, we both agree that you should not allow any non-essential cookie tracking. Maybe your Response Ranking is a 5 though.

The point of the book though, is not to change the way you utilize the online world, it is to increase that Knowledge Ranking so that you do it in a safer or more-informed manner.

Something that is rarely considered a benefit of cookies, because it isn't, is that these brief text files save information about searches and browser history that is used to target advertisers for you, and advertising and tracking is rarely for your benefit.

ADD-ONS AND EXTENSIONS

Browser add-ons and extensions can be both extremely risky and exceptionally helpful. These are small programs that allow you to use more functionality of your browser. It used to be a requirement to know how to add and configure extensions in Firefox or the browser was near useless. Today, Firefox is not only much simpler to **configure** and add **to**, but also **much more productive** and **private** with an out-of-the-box **default installation**.

My password manager extension goes on all my **browsers**. **My password manager** for **work**, is **different** than the one I use for **personal items**. If you **have** the same **requirement**, **this might** be a **solution** for you as **well**.

On my **Firefox Browser I have extensions** that are a little more **privacy-centric** like "**Facebook Container**" which **makes going** through **Facebook much easier** to **accept** for anyone with a **Response Rank** of 3 or **higher**.

Many people use a **browser extension** to **block ads** on **sites** like **YouTube**. **While not helpful** with **privacy**, it **makes** the **viewing experience much more** relaxed and ad-free. **I under**stand the **desire**, but I don't **mind paying YouTube** for the **service** to see ad-free **content**. If **Charles finds** out I **pay** $24 **a month** for **YouTube**, he **might smack me** in the **back** of the **head**.

DON'T FORGET APPS

On **computers**, **phones**, **smart TVs**, **gaming consoles**, and **other** such **devices**, you **might** do **most** of **these** web **browsing tasks** with an **app that** you **downloaded** and **signed into**. This **would replace** the **browser** on **these devices**.

Browsers, **search engines**, and **apps** (on **phones**, **smart TVs**, and now **computers** as **well**) all **have something** in **common that** you **need** to be **aware** of. **They** are **usually tracking** your **every move**.

Browsers like **Edge**, **Chrome**, **Safari**, **Firefox**, and even **Brave**, are **tracking information** on **your habits** and **history**. **Brave** and **Firefox** seem to do a lot **less with that data than** the **tech giants behind Edge** (**Microsoft**) and **Chrome** (**Alphabet** or **Google**), but **there** is **some tracking happening**.

Search Engines like **Google**, **Bing**, and **Yahoo**, also **track** **every**thing that you do. **Google** has become one of the **largest companies** on **ear**th, largely **because** of the amount of **data** that they collect and use, as well as sell. But the advent of **smartp**hones and smart **TVs** has **brought** about an additional **threat** to our **privacy** that you **need** to be **awa**re of.

Applications that you **use** on your **phone** and **TV** also **track every**thing you **type**, and **there** is an **inord**inate amount of **data showing** that these **devices themsel**ves **listen** to what we **say** even when **they aren't turned** on.

Ask some of your **friends** if they **think their phones** are **listening** to them. **Many** will have a **story** about being in a **conver**sation with someone **where** they **brought** up a **topic**, **such** as drug **runners** in **Colombia**, and **then started** seeing **advertisements** for **travelling** to **Colombia popping** up in their **sear**ches, **browsing**, and **shopping sites. They** had **never spoken** the word **Colombia**.

They had **never searched** for it. **Their phone wasn't even unlocked** when **someone else talked** about the **drug runners** in **Colombia**. Yet **here they** are, **seeing** ads for **something** that their **phone overheard someone else** say in a **conver**sation.

These stories are **not insigni**ficant, nor are they **rare**.

This invasion of our **privacy** is **not** all **bad**. Some **applic**ations are also **websi**tes. **Think** of **large sites** like **Amazon, Spotify,** and **Netf**lix. **They** have **apps** for your **phone** and **TV,** and **they** often **track every**thing that you **say** or **type**. **They** don't **store** every **piece** of **inform**ation about you to **sell** to **others. Often, they** are **collecting** the **inform**ation and **using** it to **improve their service** to you. **This inva**sion of **privacy** will **improve your** experience, **which** will **make** you **feel better** about **spending** your **money** with **them** or **giving them your data**.

Amazon revi**ews y**our shop**ping hab**its t**o sugg**est ite**ms y**ou **migh**t be **inter**ested in buy**ing** or **sugg**ests purch**asing consum**ables **you** purch**ased in t**he pa**st.

Spotify us**es y**our hist**ory of podc**asts **a**nd son**gs to sugg**est new ite**ms you migh**t like, **a**nd in my exper**ience, they** d**o a fanta**stic job at th**is… perh**aps bet**ter th**an any**one.

As a side no**te, Spot**ify is n**ow sell**ing audio**books, **a**nd **I** lo**ok forward t**o see**ing wh**at th**eir algor**ithms **sugg**est for m**e in that** are**na.** With t**he prem**ium **subscri**ption, which **I** wi**ll cont**inue pay**ing f**or ev**en now th**at the price has incre**ased in **Dece**mber of 2024, th**ere is a va**st amo**unt of 'free' books to abs**orb with m**y 15 hou**rs of free liste**ning eac**h mon**th.

Google wi**ll ta**ke yo**ur loca**tion da**ta if y**ou let th**em, b**ut in exch**ange, they let y**ou us**e Google Maps at no ch**arge. If y**ou are us**ing it f**or traf**fic, it is prob**ably t**he be**st traf**fic app in the world, mo**stly due t**o the fact they ha**ve the larg**est traf**fic data**set. Th**is is beca**use they a**re trac**king alm**ost ev**ery **Andr**oid ce**ll pho**ne **a**nd us**ing that data t**o sho**w you whe**re oth**er ce**ll ph**ones a**re trav**eling be**low the speed lim**it or stop**ped comp**letely in a road**way.

If we liv**ed in a wor**ld fil**led wi**th **A**2 peo**ple like Char**les, the Google Maps traf**fic app wo**uld be virtu**ally us**ele**ss beca**use **nob**ody wo**uld sha**re the**ir loca**tion da**ta wi**th Google Maps. **Char**les would lo**ve a wor**ld fil**led wi**th peo**ple who we**re mo**re act**ive in prote**cting the**ir priv**acy. I agr**ee with him that w**e co**uld prob**ably live in a wor**ld with**out the ben**efits of all the**se invas**ions of our priv**acy.

While I agree, I al**so enj**oy the traf**fic serv**ices of Goo**gle Maps. **Not want**ing t**o be a **hypocr**ite, I sha**re m**y ce**ll pho**ne loca**tion const**antly wi**th Google, **a**nd by prox**y, wi**th many oth**er compa**nies **I** may nev**er kn**ow abo**ut.

If you ha**ve a Netf**lix acco**unt, you may ha**ve notic**ed that the thumb**nails that y**ou see f**or y**our sho**ws **a**nd mov**ies diff**er from tho**se of your family members. Netflix thinks I will be more likely to click on a thumbnail with an explosion and my wife would be more apt to click on a romantic kiss from the same movie. They are probably correct.

OTHER LEAKS IN YOUR BOAT

There are many more ways for your personal information to leave your control than just you giving it away or browsers, search engines, and apps absconding with it.

Sometimes the devices in your home are out to get you. Not only are all the devices that you connect to your home Wi-Fi (wireless network) capable of allowing hackers access to your computers, but they also take data from your home and store it in the cloud.

Remember all the devices with minimal security systems from Chapter 2: Passwords are Stupid? Were you aware that coffee makers, refrigerators, robot vacuums, smart TVs, baby monitors, and many other devices, have been found to store information that they gather in the cloud? Would it bother you to know that if you have a TV with audio commands, everything you say in earshot of it might be uploaded to the manufacturer's web servers so they can scan the data for information?

What if they say they will never scan it but then someone decides that your family discussions should be subpoenaed for a legal issue you are having? How do you feel about audio recordings of everything spoken in front of your TV being used against you?

Anything that you connect to your home network, by cable or Wi-Fi access, is an attack entry point and a potential leak of your personal information from a vendor, hacker, or government.

This is not to convince you to stop using these devices in your home, but consider whether you need your coffee maker app on your phone so you can brew a new pot from your mobile device.

STORY TIME – VENDOR ABUSE

Before you write off this information as crazy conspiracy theories, I want you to remember the difference between a conspiracy theory and a fact... about 2 months nowadays.

On May 25, 2023, Brandon Jackson came home to realize that he was locked out of his Amazon Echo and all the technology that he had running through the Amazon smart home tools. Amazon claimed that a delivery driver heard a racial slur through his doorbell. Amazon said he was under investigation. [44]

For six days, Mr. Jackson lost access to many home devices and struggled to manually use everything from appliances and lights that we worked so hard to automate. In the end, Brandon, a black man from Maryland, was locked out of his technology because a big-tech company accused him of saying something racist.

What nobody was talking about was whether Amazon had the right to shut down his access for being a racist (which he denied). Being a racist is not illegal in the USA. You are 100% within your legal right to be a complete jerk or idiot. In America, you are supposed to be guaranteed freedom of speech. I was shocked that Amazon would disable his access to his home devices for saying something that they disagree with.

America is also home to a very litigious culture. How could Amazon get away without being sued by this man?

You need not worry. Even when Amazon gets away easy from oppressing their customers, they still have to deal with one of the most bloated bureaucracies on the planet.

---

[44] Amazon Abuse of Power
http://footnote44.dbtwl.com

STORY TIME – AMAZON GETS BUSTED

In 2023 **Amazon was busted by the FTC for spying on customers and were fined over \$30M.**[45] The fact that **Amazon employees** had **access to people's home cameras was a little creepy. The fact that so many people had cameras in their bedrooms and bathrooms proves that there are way too many people who are an F on their Knowledge Ranking or have a Response Ranking of 5, or possibly both.**

There **is more coming about cameras that you need to be aware of** in **Chapter 8: A Fresh Can of Spam.**

I **have to bring up the difference again between the Knowledge Rank and Response Rank. Now that you have read this far, no matter how little you knew about technology before, you can never consider yourself an F moving forward. Unless of course you didn't understand anything you read.**

The **point is that you are learning things with every page and even though Charles and I already know all these things, there is very little chance that he will ever connect a coffee maker or vacuum to his home Wi-Fi. If he did, it would be on a separate wireless network and locked out from the network where his family computers are residing. Whereas I recently purchased a space heater for the sole purpose of connecting it to my wireless network.**

In **the winter, I don't get out to my trailer at the lake very often. I reduce my visits from every single weekend all summer to once a month if I am lucky in the winter. The problem is if I go out there on a Friday night when the temperature is -20C (-4F for our American readers), the trailer won't be warm for 10 to 20 hours. With the new heater, I'll be able to log into it and turn it on the day before I arrive.**

---

[45] Amazon Employees Spying on Customers
http://footnote45.dbtwl.com

If I were into ice fishing, I would probably own two of these.

Even Charles couldn't hold this against me. But I'm not telling him about it, just in case.

PLAY ALONG

In this chapter's Play Along section, your browser is going to become more secure and less of your data will leave you unknowingly.

Task 5-1 Install Brave

You don't need to use Brave but I really want you to install the browser both as practice and also to make it available if you decide to try it out in the future. Go to www.brave.com and click on "Download Brave" from the top right corner. Go through the installation process and then choose whether you want to 'test' Brave or set it as your default web browser.

Task 5-2 Stop Saving Stuff

Open each browser and go to the "Settings" tab.

From Chrome settings, on the left menu, click on "Autofill and Passwords", then "Google Password Manager" and in "Settings" turn off "Offer to save passwords". Then go back to "Payment methods" (might be in another tab) and turn that off as well. You also need to go back one and click on "Addresses and more" and stop saving and auto-filling in your name and address.

For Edge, click on "Profiles" on the left menu and then under "Personal info" turn off "Save and fill basic info". Under "Passwords" turn off everything that saves anything. Under "Payment info" disable "save and fill payment info".

For Brave, click on the "Autofill and passwords". Click on "Password Manager" then "Settings" and disable "Offer to save passwords" and "Sign in automatically". Click on "Payment methods" and disable everything and then back to "Addresses and more" and uncheck "Save and fill addresses.

The exercise of going through the Settings menus on your browsers is more than most people will ever do. Knowing what you already know, I can't imagine that anyone could ever think that they haven't gotten their money's worth out of this book already.

As an aside, we should mention that now many credit card companies are putting your name, card number, expiration date, and Card Verification Value (The CVV code) on the back of the card, this will make it more likely that someone will steal your card info when you pull it out.

Task 5-3 Browser Test

Go to our www.DontBeTheWeakestLink.com website or go to www.DBTWL.com to test your browser security. Under "The Book" > Chapter 5 > Play Along

You will see a "Browser Test" link. Open this link in each of your browsers and see how they compare.

After going through this task, write down some of your key findings below and if you have any questions, make a note as well and post them to me on your favorite social media platform or on our website under the Contact Us menu.

Task 5-4 Mobile Ears

We want to show you how your mobile device is listening to you even when you are not asking or expecting it to.

What you need to do several times a day is say one of the countries on the list below so that your phone can hear you. Do not turn on the audio recorder or any application. Just have your phone on and repeat the country several times a day for a week or so.

The result should be that Google or Apple has started selling your interest in the country to advertising companies and you should start seeing references to it online. Be sure to choose a country that you don't regularly say, for example:

- Estonia
- Madagascar
- Tasmania

CHAPTER 6: SECURITY 2.0

Now that you know what makes a password or passphrase great (making it long, complex, and never duplicated), it seems like a good time to dig a little deeper. Let's discuss some advanced security ideas, or Security 2.0 (pronounced 'two point oh' for those non-techies). I just realized how funny that is going to sound in the audiobook version. I liked this chapter title because it sounded nerdy, and that's the way I roll.

There are several methods of implementing advanced security and you are likely familiar with one or two of them already. Typically, these solutions frustrate you because they "waste" your time, but we would like to change that perception. Whenever your bank or email provider makes you jump through a few hoops to log in, remember that these hoops are also required if some hacker in Malaysia tries to log in.

TTT - TOP HACKER LOCATIONS

I am not picking on one country here out of some bigoted social perceptions. I am randomly choosing countries with high numbers of infiltration attacks, and it would get boring quickly if I blamed everything on Russia or China, especially when two of the worst hacks I have ever been involved with came from Malaysia and Turkey.

Go to the Chapter 6 Time Travel Tips on our website to learn more.

BOT CHECKS

Do you remember when we talked about your password being harder to guess?

To make sure that people are doing the guessing, and not other computers, you will often see a bot-checker on your login screen. It can be a simple check box that says, "I am not a robot" or "I am a real person". Without getting side-tracked with a Pinocchio joke, you must understand that threat actors have programmed computers to check these boxes. Can't you just picture that little guy on strings pushing buttons... "I am a real boy!"

Sites started asking you to retype a code that was buried in a picture, a cluster of scribbles, or colored dots that made it more and more difficult for people with poor eyesight to log into their services. Some sites started showing you a photo of numbers and letters that were difficult for computers to scan.

This progressed into the nine small boxes of pictures where you were asked to click on the photos with traffic lights, vehicles, signs, etc. I don't mind this, but I agree with the people who complain that the apps don't seem to know what images have traffic lights or crosswalks. Sometimes I have to click on four different sets of photos because it thinks I don't know what a motorcycle looks like.

You obviously care about your privacy and securing your information, or you wouldn't be reading this book. I would encourage you to think differently about these intrusions in your time. Rather than being annoyed by a site that makes you jump through a hoop to log in, watch for sites that do not make you jump through any hoops and ask yourself why they don't value your personal information.

2FA OR MFA

We have tried to limit the number of acronyms that are used in the book because the computer world uses more acronyms than an MSN chat room (that's the Microsoft Network). Do millennials even know what chat rooms are? At any rate, we decided 2FA had to be included in the book because it might change the way you feel about security, and I am also fond of the technology and the acronym.

2FA stands for Two-Factor Authentication. It is also referred to as MFA, or Multi-Factor Authentication. There are five common authentication factors that can verify you...

1. Who you are
2. What you have
3. What you know
4. Where you are
5. When you are there

When two of these factors are used to prove who you are, you are using 2FA. You are always welcome to use more factors and although 2FA is a type of MFA, typically anything requiring over two factors is called MFA.

Who you are can be a fingerprint, retina scan, voice recognition, face recognition, etc. These are the physical parts of you that can't be changed.

What you have could be a bank card, security badge, key fob, or cell phone.

What you know is usually a password, PIN, or security hint.

Where you are could be a geographical location, restricted computer, or a pre-configured computer IP address.

When you are there could be restricted by login schedules or time zones for local resources.

The most abundant form of 2FA that you are probably familiar with, is your bank card or credit card PIN. Financial institutions love this because it requires a physical card as well as a PIN that you have locked away in your head. Something *you have* AND *something you know*. 2FA.

Unless you are one of those people who wrote their PIN on the back of your card. In that case, we would still be dealing with single factor authentication because anyone who had your card would also know what you know, your PIN.

Of course, so many people complained it was difficult to remember the PIN all the time, that credit card companies now allow you to simply tap a credit card for purchases under specific limits.

Do not look at the PIN as an obstacle for you to buy something. Look at it as an obstacle for someone else to steal something from you.

We have observed that implementing 2FA improves as technology usage increases. As soon as humans are involved, the system breaks down. If you ever phone the government or a bank and they ask you to verify who you are, this is NOT necessarily a form of 2FA but they look at it as if it is. You have their phone number. That proves nothing. You have a credit card or account number. That proves nothing.

While I understand the personal questions and confirming that I know my account number, I think it makes a mockery of the security process if hackers can find all the answers to their questions on my last monthly bill or my Facebook profile. Call me crazy, but how does me knowing my birthday prove to you I am me? Who doesn't know my birthday? For the record, it is not January 1.

It would be so much easier if the person on the phone sent you a text or email and asked you to click on a link. That would verify that you had possession of the cell phone or email account that they had for you, as well as the account number from a statement.

THE DREADED TEXT

Most people have had to type a 6-digit code from their cell phone into a website by now. After telling you how much this adds to your security as a true MFA solution, I need to warn you that it is not even close to foolproof.

Hackers use this to compromise us by telling us that they are sending us a code to verify who we are... they text us a code and ask us for the number to prove that we are the person who we claim to be. This puts us on the defensive and blinds us to the fact that they are not to be trusted. Give those texted numbers to nobody, ever.

The fact is that while they are convincing us that they are the bank by telling us our address and phone number they are on our login page trying to reset our password. When the website says they will send us a code to prove who we are, we then give it to a hacker on the phone.

I left one of the big five banks in Canada and moved all my business away from them because this was part of their legitimate customer service. Every time I called in, we would get to the point where they texted me a code and asked me to read it back.

I would shake my head and tell them that they needed to find another way. I have seen a few companies do this and I tell them every time that they are reading from the 'hacker's handbook' and I refuse to humor them. It has cost me time and money, but I refuse to deal with companies that have such insecure business practices even though I understand that they think they are using a system that enhances their security.

> I will not condone a company I deal with,
> trying to enhance their security, by putting mine at risk.

MFA APPS

You may be familiar with MFA applications for your phone. They are used to replace the six-digit codes texted to your phone that allow you to login to a website or application. If you are not using one, you should be, because they are much more secure than texts to your cell phone.

There are many choices with the apps. Of course, the big companies have their own, Google Authenticator and Microsoft Authenticator, and Authy is a large competitor in the space. My preference is 2FAS, and because of its simplicity and flexibility, it is the app I use for all my client accounts.

MFA apps are more flexible and secure than texts because you can install extensions in your browser, so you don't need a phone to work online. When you log onto a website and it asks for a code, simply click on the extension and copy the code. You can quickly paste the code and authenticate yourself.

The authentication app allows you to sort your accounts into folders, so you don't need to scroll through all your accounts to get to the one you are looking for. They have another feature that we really think you need to turn on for increased security. If you are a 5, and maybe even a 4 on the Response Ranking, then you might not need this, but anyone from 1 to 3 will want to hear this warning.

Mobile devices are a tremendous security risk. Phones get lost and stolen much more frequently than laptops and computers. We will talk more about phones in **Chapter 11: Hitting Closer to Home**.

You should always lock your phone with a PIN or shape and also set a PIN for your MFA app, ensuring that the two PINs are different.

One thing that the world doesn't seem to take into consideration yet, but I am sure it is coming, is that MFA applications may confirm authentication on the same device as the service. It is the same problem with text messages but without a solution yet.

If you secure your online shopping account so that you cannot log in without MFA, but then set it up on an app on your phone, anyone who steals your phone can open your shopping app and then the app security will text you a code... to your phone that was just stolen. Boom, free shopping.

Charles and I would be happy to see your security look like this... your phone has a 7-digit PIN to unlock it, and your shopping site requires a 6-digit code from an MFA app, and your MFA app has its own 4-digit PIN to access it. Nobody can use your shopping site on your phone without knowing two codes and typing in a third code.

> If you use text as MFA or an unsecured MFA app,
> to secure an app or service you are accessing on your phone, then you
> DO NOT have MFA.

SECURE HINTS (OR PASSWORD HINTS)

Yesterday I was talking about secure password hints with one of my favorite clients. Let's call her Sheila. Password hints are the questions that you set up with your bank or email provider when you create an account where you select three questions from a short list and then give them the answers. The questions often look like "What is your mother's maiden name?", "What city were you born in?",

"What was your first car?", or "Who was your favorite childhood superhero?".

These questions should only have one answer, which is one reason I dislike them. Companies think they are good security tools and simple to use, but I changed my favorite childhood superhero at least once a year growing up.

Sites believe these hints are secure for a few reasons:

    1. You choose the questions, and thus they are regarded as personal and random.

    2. The answers are personal.

    3. The answers may vary immensely and are random.

What these people don't realize is that the things that make secure hints so secure can also be significant security flaws.

The first problem is this, although you choose the questions from a list of up to 20 or more, this is far from random. I recall those questions so easily above because they are the same questions asked on dozens of sites. This is not even close to what random means.

If I use the same three or four questions on all my sites, the effectiveness of the "secure hints" ends the moment one of those sites is compromised and everyone knows my answers to those questions. If I am unaware of this security flaw, or if I am unaware that the site has been compromised, then I am living with a false sense of security that is at least as perilous as having only a password.

At least with no "random" questions, I would know my personal information was potentially up for grabs and I would protect other avenues of attack by making sure my password was great.

The second point was that the answers were personal, but once again, once those "personal" answers are out there in the open, their security value drops to zero.

The third point is that the answers varied **immen**sely. **I cannot argue** that **my mother's maiden** name **could** be **virtu**ally any **combin**ation of letters of any **length,** but once **a hacker knows my** mother's real **maiden** name, I am **vulnerable. What** are the **chances** that you varied your **responses between** two **sites? Alm**ost **zero.**

Your **mother's maiden** name is, and was, and **always** will be, the same **answer.** Once **this answer** has been **compromised,** it is **worthless.**

That was, **until today.**

YOUR MOTHER'S NEW MAIDEN NAME

I am **going** to give you **a rather simple solution that** will **make your** password **hints virtually bulletproof.** In your **password manager,** there is **probably a field** for **notes where** you can **enter anything.** What **I always do** is **type my password hints in this area.**

No, I **don't need help** to **remember** the **actual answers** to the **questions. Well, I do now, but I don't need** to **remember my mother's** maiden name, not her **real** one **anyway.**

Yesterday, I was **showing Sheila how** to **resolve** the **insecurity of** password **hints** in this **exact fashion.** The **questions came up, and I** told **her** to **select a question. It mattered little which question it was** and was **oddly more secure** if it was a **question** she had **never chosen** on a site **before.** She **chose** "What is your **city of birth?".**

I told **her** to **look around her office** and **tell me** the **first thing that** she saw.

A **prompt reply came,** "A **large green plant".**

I told **her** to **type that into** the **answer.**

"For **my city of bir**th?"

I **grinned** at her, and she **typed it.**

The next question was chosen, "What is your favorite sport?". I didn't think Sheila was a big sports enthusiast, so this may have been the first time that she ever chose this question.

I told her to type in the same answer, "A large green plant".

I don't recall what the third question was, but can you guess what the answer was?

You got it… "A large green plant".

In her password manager, she put the following note… "HINT: A large green plant"

If she ever needed to reset her password or prove her identity, she simply needed to open her password manager and she knew the answer to every question.

It is convenient if they are all the same, but some sites require different answers for each question.

Here is a huge security bonus. If that site was ever compromised and those answers were stolen, they would be useless to any other site because Sheila no longer chooses the same questions every time and her answers are never the same between sites. Let us look again at the three password hint security features.

1. The questions are chosen by you, so they are personal and random.

We have proven that these questions are not secure once compromised but now they are more random because you really don't care what the questions are. You might not even be reading them. You are randomly choosing one of the dozen questions because you don't care what the question is or what the real answer is.

2. The **answers** are **pers**onal.

The **answers** are **no longer only** extremely **pers**onal, **but also environ**mental and **usually** don't even **make sen**se. The **answers** reflect **something physical in front** of you at the **moment** you **choose** the **password hint. That item might** not **be there a week later** if **someone** moved a **plant, or it died, as it would in my off**ice. **You might** not even **be in your off**ice **when you had to choose these quest**ions **ne**xt.

3. The **answers vary immen**sely.

Under the **old answers, the city you were born in could have been** one of **thous**ands of **cities but now it could be something much more unique,** like...

- **A large green plant**
- **2 Sticky Note pads**
- **4 pieces of Gum!**

I **think you get the idea.**

For the record, **those other answers above are all some that I remember choosing in the recent past. You may notice that I still try to include all four character-types and a lengthy answer.**

Your password hints in the future will now be infinitely **more** secure **than they ever have been in the past.**

Many sites now require **unique answers for each of the hints. I hope that this wasn't something of my doing. I now add something** to the **end of each answer if it is requ**ired:

- **City of birth: Large green plant city**
- **Mother's maiden name: Large green plant name**
- **First car: Large green plant car**

I **then document all three in the pass**word **mana**ger.

STORY TIME – GOVERNOR PALIN

In 2008, Alaska Governor Sarah Palin had her personal email hacked. What kind of training and skill did the hacker possess to perform this skilled breach?

He didn't use much at all. He simply got Yahoo to reset her password by answering three questions (Sarah's secure hints). A couple minutes with a search engine and he knew where she was born, her zip code, and where she met her husband.[46]

In a recent interview the hacker found online, Sarah Palin stated that she met her husband at high school. A quick search found she graduated from Wasilla High. And that was how easy it was.

There was nothing top secret in her personal email but there were some government emails and she was all about transparency. It did not look good that she had a personal Yahoo email account to conduct any government business. It also did not look good that she was hacked while running for Vice President.

THE TROUBLE WITH BIOLOGY

You probably do not know what biology has to do with protecting your privacy, but it is becoming increasingly more prevalent in our security practices. You may recall that one of the five factors of authentication is "who you are". "Who you are" is your biology, and these are some ways that we use it today:

- **Finger**print
- Voice **recogni**tion
- Retina scan

---

[46] Sarah Palin Hack
http://footnote46.dbtwl.com

- **Face recognition**

There are other methods as well, but these are the most common. You can also use combinations of these, but since we won't be discussing accessing top secret labs, we can stick with single uses.

If you have never used any of these "biometric" methods of authentication to log into a phone or a laptop, then you probably know someone who has. These login methods are becoming more commonplace every day, but I am not a huge fan of biometric authentication for a few reasons.

The first is the obvious one that you have read stories about. Before we go any further, I want you to know that my wife has 100% access to every personal device and login on my phone and laptop.

Access without your knowledge is a problem. How many stories have you heard about a cheating husband getting busted because his wife unlocked his phone while he was sleeping by touching it to his finger or holding it in front of his face? These biological things do not change if you are sleeping and that is a security problem and not just because I don't want my wife to read my texts.

If you are drunk, sleeping, or otherwise incapacitated, people should not be able to use a part of "you" to authenticate to any device or service.

Biometrics is not the security people think it is.

It should scare you that two of my sons, born over a decade apart, can open the same iPhone with facial recognition. It scares me. I have heard comedians that can sound exactly like people and with the new AI technology, should voice recognition even qualify as MFA?

With AI, we will undoubtedly hear a lot more about hacks involving a phone call where voice recognition was used to authenticate or prove that the caller was the real person. Not only could an AI voicemail convince a friend or relative to e-transfer some money, but many financial institutions now use voice recognition to authenticate you.

We can get into that more in **Chapter 9: Smooth Criminals**.

While we might have given permission for them to use voice recognition out of convenience, we should know this is NOT a stronger security measure than five questions about us or our account.

STORY TIME – QATAR FLIGHT TO BALI

The story that keeps popping into my head is the Qatar flight to Bali that made an emergency landing in India to drop off a woman and her drunk husband and son because she unlocked his phone while he slept and a few minutes later started beating him for cheating on her.[47]

I bet that guy wishes he had a numeric code or swipe shape to unlock his phone now, but I find it hard to feel bad for him. He threw away his marriage long before getting on that flight, and now he has a $50,000 bill to pay to the airline for the emergency landing.

Sure, there are more significant reasons to not depend on biometrics for security, but how Wesley Snipes used biometrics in Demolition Man is not realistically something you need to worry about.[48]

---

[47] Qatar flight to Bali
http://footnote47.dbtwl.com
[48] Demolition Man prison escape
http://footnote48.dbtwl.com

For those who do not get the movie reference, Wesley Snipes broke out of prison by using the warden's eyeball on a retina scan. Let your imagination paint a picture. It was a great movie if you only watched it for the three seashells or to see President Schwarzenegger (long before he became Governor of California in the real world).

A scorned wife holding a phone to the finger of a cheating husband as he sleeps is probably not reason enough to dump biometrics, unless of course, you're the cheating husband. Some might call it a reason to support biometrics but, it is a method of bypassing security, and Charles and I do not endorse biometrics as a security measure at this time (unless your employment requires it).

There is a much more significant issue with biometric authentication. What if someone ever compromised the sites that store your biometric data?

That "if" made clients wary years ago when I started making users use different fingers for every device. In 2004 when our office received our first tablet that had a biometric fingerprint scanner. I told users to use their index finger on their right to log into their laptop, their thumb for their second device, and now they could have ten devices with independent credentials. If any credentials were ever compromised, the users would only lose one fingerprint, and their other devices would remain secure.

> Using the same finger, voice, face, etc.
> to access two devices or services.
> is the biometric equivalent to reusing the same password.

We all have a knowledge rank high enough to know that we should never use the same password more than once. If you didn't know this before picking up this book, you should know it now.

STORY TIME – SUPREMA BIOSTAR 2 COMPROMISE

There is no longer a doubt that biological credentials might be stolen. Hackers have already compromised biometric data, with a significant breach with the exposure of Suprema's Biostar 2 dataset in 2019. This dataset had over 27 million records, included biometric logins for building access in 83 countries with clients from banks, governments, and the UK Metropolitan Police.[49]

I have a tremendous problem with biometrics being stolen because you can't change your face or fingerprint. If your password gets stolen, you can easily log in and change it. How do you recover from the theft of your face? There is a John Travolta and Nicholas Cage joke in here somewhere.[50]

There are other issues I have because electronics and software can easily fool the input devices. And it's usually easier than pulling a password or PIN out of your head. Now, anyone can purchase all those ones and zeros that enable a computer to recognize your face, your fingerprint, or your voice. That cannot make you feel secure while you sleep at night.

When I first started dealing with biometrics over 20 years ago, I had users limiting loss to a single finger per device, but what if you used your face, voice, or eyeball? You cannot change your face like you change your password. How many times can someone steal your biological data before you become a security risk to your company?

---

[49] Suprema Biostar 2 exposure
http://footnote49.dbtwl.com
[50] Face/Off trailer
http://footnote50.dbtwl.com

Don't forget to always put a note in your password program as to what biometric data a device or site has access to. If they get compromised, you can always refer back to determine which part of you was compromised and avoid using it again.

Biometrics is one topic where Charles and I are in close agreement. I am hesitant to use biometrics, but when the US border agent asked for my handprint and retina scan to gain a Nexus card, it didn't take me long to submit. I weighed the benefits of never standing in a security line at an airport, against handing over my biometrics, and decided in about 3 seconds that I had no concerns trading my fingerprints and retina scan for that wonderful little card.

I could probably convince Charles to do the same, but it would take significantly longer than 3 seconds. Because he doesn't fly as often as I do, the benefits of avoiding long lines would not be as clear cut either. I have to give my fingerprints to our national police service every two years and have done so for the past few of decades to get a PRC (Police Record Check). This allows me to volunteer with a local children's festival, our local church, Scouts Canada, and Search and Rescue. I have also needed that same check many times for projects for my consulting career.

While Charles would still be significantly more hesitant to give his biometric data to anyone, he understands that government agencies rely on such information to quickly prove or disprove a person's identity. We both agree that government agencies put way too much value on insecure measures and few of them do enough to protect their data.

Keep in mind though, now that the US government has my retina scan, I would never use it again for something important because I would never trust that the US government wouldn't lose it, sell it, or give it away to someone for political gain. The thought of them using it themselves has also crossed my mind, even before Charles brought it up.

One last issue I have with biometrics is that they are significantly less convenient if you have a bandaid on your finger, dirty hands or if the weather has forced you to wear gloves, scarfs or something warm to cover your body.

Gloves and scarves are probably not issues in India, but I wanted to make mention of India because they have the largest open biometrics system in the world. I say "open" because I honestly have no idea if secretive government programs exist in countries like The USA or China that may have taken more data points on their citizens than India.

In under 12 years, India has had 1.3 billion people (three times the population of the USA) voluntarily enroll in a program where they add biometric data to their national ID. Currently, they enroll with fingerprints and retinal scans, effectively erasing duplicate and fake ID scams in one of the largest countries on the planet.[51]

Shopping chain, Costco, has recently started scanning cards at the entry to ensure that only rightful card holders are entering their stores. This isn't biometrics per se, but they are clearly using my face for more than they initially did when they took my photo.

I also want to say that a few of my clients have used palm scanners to log employee attendance and I have never seen a more secure way of ensuring that two employees aren't clocking in and out for one another to game their employer. As much as Charles and I dislike this practice, neither of us have seen a better alternative.

CREDIT CARD

Credit card companies seem to be infatuated with poor security practices. We have already talked about the "genius" of allowing people to tap a credit card (did you catch the sarcasm?).

---

[51] India's Aadhaar biometric ID
http://footnote51.dbtwl.com

Shayne Kawalilak   CHAPTER 6: SECURITY 2.0

To my knowledge, no one has ever hacked the chip included in new credit cards. We also have the ability to force 2FA or MFA by still requiring a PIN. But every credit card still has something on it I cannot explain… your name.

I can't for the life of me think of a single reason to have your name on a credit card. The only person aided by this is a criminal. I do not know one other person in the world who cares about your name.

If you stick that card in a machine, and you enter a PIN, you have provided proof to the store and the credit card company that you are authorized to use that card. If you used the PIN to verify the purchase with two-factor authentication, there is no way for you to dispute this charge. No merchants care about your name. They only care that the credit card supplier approves the charge.

A little caveat here because, for some strange reason, many stores in the US still ask for ID or a signature with credit cards. There is no point in asking for ID without checking the names match on both cards. There is no point in asking for a signature if you don't confirm it looks comparable to the one on the card.

I have signed many credit card slips in the US and never had anyone compare it to the signature that does not exist on the back of my credit card.

I have not traveled to any place that requires a signature in years, except for the USA. Charles can't remember the last time someone asked him to sign a slip with a purchase.

Don't Be the Weakest Link   Page 139

PLAY ALONG

For this chapter, we are going to install an MFA app on your phone. Feel free to uninstall the app once you complete the book, or keep it on your phone until you require it.

You can find the specific steps on our website at www.DontBeTheWeakestLink.com or www.DBTWL.com. Click on "The Book" in the top menu and then "Chapter 6" and "Play Along".

Once you have installed the MFA application as per the webpage, we need to go to the security settings and enable the PIN. Ensure that the PIN you choose is NOT the same as the PIN for your phone.

From this point on, you only need to rely on insecure texting codes for sites that do not inherently value the security of your data.

_____

_____

_____

_____

_____

_____

_____

_____

_____

_____

CHAPTER 7: IS ANTI-VIRUS ENOUGH

I suppose since the world has been telling you how important anti-virus software is, I should spend a little time explaining why I don't think it is enough. One of the most popular questions at my presentations is, "what is my favorite anti-virus application?".

My simple answer is, "yes".

"What do you mean 'yes' is your favorite?", is the typical follow-up.

I end up explaining that yes, I believe anti-virus software is my favorite, if the choice is having it or not having it. At different times in my career I have recommended vendors from McAfee, Kaspersky, Sophos, Webroot, Bitdefender, etc.

The speed at which exploits are found and updated in the software became much more important when it seemed like there was a new digital epidemic each few months. Today I still think it is important, but probably not the threat that the ransomware and phishing threats are to my clients (more talk about them coming soon).

Tomorrow may hold an unknown threat that takes the top spot in my priorities, but for the writing of this book, I wanted to let you know something about the options that are available to you right now in 2024, well, 2025 in a couple weeks.

WHAT IS ANTI-VIRUS?

There are thousands of viruses that could infect your computer. Anti-virus (or AV) solutions range in price from free to $50 per month. They range in efficacy from effective to near useless, some are even harmful. I simply recommend that you use one of them. Keep in mind that there are also AV solutions out there whose purpose is to infect your system with viruses.

This should remind you to always get your software from a reputable source. A full 20% of the computers that I personally support use the free protection provided by Microsoft Windows called Windows Defender. Is it the best option available? Probably not. But this is a subjective opinion of something that might change tomorrow.

Here is what I do know. If me saving you a few dollars on anti-virus software helps to convince you to purchase a second layer of defense like a firewall or malware solution, then I call it a win and I am more than satisfied with the free application that Microsoft supplies.

TTT – ANTI-VIRUS RANKINGS

I want to mention here that websites ranking hardware and software online require more education and experience than most things you will see in this book. Most of the reviews that you find accept paid reviews from vendors for placement or are outright owned by a vendor. Charles and I will add our personal knowledge and experience to the TTT lists in this chapter.

Our choice will prioritize these features valued in this order...

1. **Protection quality**
2. **Affordability**
3. Low **performance overhead** on the **computer**
4. Low **up sell marketing**
5. **Additional feature availability**

Our top pick overall is **Bitdefender.**[52]

THE FIREWALL

The firewall is not the only security that you need, but it is important enough for me to state that if you don't have one, you better have all your other security ducks in a row.

If you take your work laptop home, or work remotely, and spend as much time online at your house as you do at the office, or even more when you consider the weekend, doesn't it make sense that you would put the same effort into protecting your devices at home as you do at the office? I am not saying you need the same high-end firewall that you have at the workplace, but I am saying you should have a firewall. It makes sense that you should not leave your data protection to the free home router your ISP (Internet Service Provider) provided.

Once again, I have supported and promoted many firewalls over the years and almost any firewall is better than no firewall.

---

[52] Top Anti-Virus
http://footnote52.dbtwl.com

TTT – HOME FIREWALL RANKINGS

Our top choice for a home firewall device is the Ubiquiti USG.[53]

WHAT ABOUT MALWARE?

Malware is a much different beast than viruses, even though many people interchange the words when they really shouldn't. Viruses are considered malware because they are infections that are intended to spread, and malware encompasses any unwanted software.

Nobody speaks about viruses being a type of malware because they are so prevalent that they typically get their own category. If we all know that anti-virus software stops viruses, and viruses are a type of malware, will those same programs stop all malware? Not even close.

Some solutions are decent, and they try, but it is important to understand that not all malware can be described as viruses. They also include trojans, pups (which are Potentially Unwanted Programs), key loggers, crypto-applications, spyware, adware, and basically any application that you did not mean to install.

So, what stops malware?

Anti-malware software would be the correct answer. Do you need both? I would ask you if you wanted protection from both. In my experience, anti-malware programs do not do a great job with viruses and anti-virus applications really miss the boat with the malware that doesn't fall into the virus category.

I will apologize up front because it is not the best example out there and it is not entirely accurate. For someone who really doesn't know the difference between the two, I have used this example for years and it defines the risk quite well.

---

[53] Top Home Firewall Device
http://footnote53.dbtwl.com

I will relate this to home security. The virus is the burglar who smashes a window and grabs stuff. He then runs to your neighbors and smashes their window. This is a virus, spreading until it's stopped, but he often leaves valuable items alone in a one-track pursuit of smashing and grabbing what he sees first.

Malware plans a heist, gets into your home, steals your high-end valuables and leaves, often without you knowing when they broke in.

Malware can give remote users access to your device and accounts and steal almost any information that you store on your device. Malware can also be as harmless as a pop up in your browser.

Regardless of what malware you are most likely to be infected by, anti-virus programs and malware programs have each been designed to target specific infections. You should have a separate anti-virus program protecting you from the spread of viruses and an anti-malware program protecting you from trojans, spyware, and adware. It is just a smart decision in our opinion.

TTT – MALWARE RANKINGS

Our favorite malware scan and removal tool is Malwarebytes.[54]

Charles and I agree that the two greatest effects on your computer security are your knowledge and layering. Layer different security as much as reasonable. A home computer that you check email on might get away with free AV from Windows.

> Security on your computer comes down to two things: knowledge and layering.

---

[54] Malware Ranking
http://footnote54.dbtwl.com

An office with 10 **computers** should **definitely** **have** anti-virus and anti-malware software installed. Once a company surpasses 10 computers, or has deeper security needs, they should layer a firewall on top of the two applications installed on the computers.

Layering security features is one of the most effective security practices that I have seen. It prevents skilled hackers from bypassing one feature and then walking in easily.

As for the knowledge, you are taking care of that by reading this book. Many companies bring speakers in for training, workshops, or corporate events, in order to try to increase the knowledge of their entire team with a single effort (insert shameless plug for www.ShayneKawalilak.com or www.RedFlagIT.com).

If you know another public speaker or presentation covering similar topics to this book, please let us know so that we can start promoting them as well.

OPERATING SYSTEM IMPACT

We will not get into a debate about which operating systems are better or worse overall, but I am going to speak briefly about my personal beliefs on the subject.

In the future, this chapter will probably need to be written as physical hardware usage continues to move from desktops and laptops to phones and tablets, but most of the malware is currently aimed at the larger, less mobile devices and that will be our focus.

Linux, as an operating system, currently occupies less than 5% of computers in the world. It is one of the most secure operating systems. One of the reasons is because it is open source. This means anyone can see the code behind the curtain. While this makes it vulnerable to hacking, the combination of low market share, simplicity, and a robust community of developers makes it difficult for hackers to cause much harm, but not impossible. [55]

Windows is the opposite of simplicity. The sheer number of lines of code required to give you all those pretty bells and whistles makes the Windows operating system inheritably insecure. Where Linux has no central management and everyone can see the code in the back end, Windows is owned and managed by Microsoft and the coding is locked down like the Colonel's secret recipe.

Microsoft may not be the best security company on the planet, but they are an enormous company doing a decent job. More importantly, they have a lot to lose by doing a poor job, so they spend a ton of money protecting Windows users.

The largest problem with the security of Windows stems from its success. With over 70% of the world's computers running Windows, what operating system do you think hackers are targeting most often?

To put it in perspective, Apple's market share is equal to every other vendor beneath them combined. Microsoft Windows is five times larger than Apple.

Apple used to own an 80% market share back in the 1980's but as of 2024 they are down to just over 15%. If this ever changes, I suspect Apple will be hammered by the malware and viruses in the same way Windows has been.

---

[55] Linux Hack
http://footnote55.dbtwl.com

TTT – OPERATING SYSTEM RANKINGS

While operating system market share has dramatically shifted over the past 30-40 years, we also need to watch the shift of hardware and operating systems, 10 years ago, Android barely existed and today, 2% of all computers and 71% of all phones operate on Google's Android platform.

Operating System Rankings

Computers (2024-01)	
Windows	73%
Apple OS X	16%
Linux	4%
Chrome	2%

Computers (2010-01)	
Windows	94%
Apple OS X	5%

Operating System Rankings

Mobile (2024-01)	
Android	70%
Apple OS X	29%

Mobile (2010-01)	
Symbian	34%
Apple IOS	33%
Blackberry	10%
Android	5%
Other	18%

TTT – DEVICE RANKINGS

As more information gets stored on the internet, people will only increase their browsing activities. As device usage moves from computers to mobile devices, we need to be aware of this shift and how it can affect our personal information.

Desktop vs. Mobile Rankings

Devices (2024-01)

Mobile	73%
Desktop	16%

Devices (2017-01)

Mobile	50%
Desktop	45%

Devices (2010-01)

Mobile	2%
Desktop	98%

We will talk more about mobile security in **Chapter 11 – Hitting Closer to Home**.

The most important advice I can give you, and I honestly don't see this changing in the next 20 years, is to remember to update whatever you use for security.

Microsoft is pushing hard to convince everyone to upgrade their Windows 10 computers to Window 11, and for a while, doing the upgrade on their own, without asking. Windows 11 is a much more secure operating system than Windows 10 was. The new hardware requirements make it hard to push to a small business as they will get Windows 11 when they upgrade their computers.

STORY TIME – EMAIL HACK

I want to tell you a personal story about this chapter. I had to deal with so much of this chapter with one client in early 2021.

This client called me complaining that their email wasn't working. It was discovered that three of their email accounts had been suspended because they were sending a large amount of spam out of Malaysia.

After changing the passwords on the accounts and getting their emails working again, I started scanning the computers with access to the accounts. There was no malware or evidence of intrusion on any computer, but three days later, they were all compromised again.

I made the same changes, did more digging, and told the owner I really suspected his laptop of being ground zero for the attacks.

A week later, I was resetting passwords again. Since we were already in talks about upgrading his laptop to Windows 10, I suggested I take his laptop for the night and put in a brand-new hard drive with Windows 10 just to be sure that no unwanted programs (malware) came from his Windows 7 profile.

After getting it all setup, I was copying his documents from the old hard drive to the new one and the free Windows defender software stopped me from copying a few files because malware infected them.

I had three files that were previously scanned and cleared by Windows Defender and another highly effective AV program. They were also cleared by two admirable anti-malware applications.

The only difference between the two computers was the operating system. Somehow, this malware had hidden in Windows 7, and remained undetected by virtually anything I scanned it with. Even if you do everything "right", there may still be a way for things to go sideways on you.

PLAY ALONG

If you already have anti-virus and anti-malware applications, you are off the hook for this chapter.

If in doubt, play along and let's see how much fun we can have...

Task 7-1 Install Anti-Malware Application

1. Go to our www.DontBeTheWeakestLink.com website or www.DBTWL.com and then click on The Book > Chapter 7 > then select Play Along > 7.1.

2. Select the operating system you are using and follow the instructions. They will direct you to install a free trial of an anti-malware application.

3. Once installed, run a complete scan. This may take some time, but you will still be able to use your computer while it is scanning.

I sincerely hope that the scan finds nothing, but it is unlikely that there was no malware at all. Happy hunting.

_____

_____

_____

_____

_____

_____

_____

CHAPTER 8: A FRESH CAN OF SPAM

In 1999, I was working as an IT professional in a large company with over 5000 employees. To do my job, I had to sign up for so many events and websites that some days I felt like someone had put my email address on a bathroom wall in Grand Central Station under a bold, "Email for a good time".

THE NATURE OF THE IT INDUSTRY.

I want to look back twenty years with fond memories but also with joy that technology has brought us to a much better place. Medically? It would be better to suffer from a disease or break a bone today than at any time in our history. Transportation? Cars are stronger, safer, and more luxurious. We could do this all day, but in the end, we would have to face the reality that technology has improved our quality of life virtually everywhere.

Charles would point out here, and I would have to agree with him, that technology has all but erased privacy. It has allowed too many ways to lose your personal information without your permission or knowledge.

The speed of advancing technology has made it easier for evil to spread as well. In the wonderful year of 2000, I was working with a great guy named Dyrek and spam was one of the most persistent complaints to the IT department. On occasions, we complained as much as the users we were supporting.

Of course, our complaints fell on deaf ears because we could only complain to one another.

NATURAL PROGRESSION

As end users of technology, we need to slow down with our adoption of everything new. I don't want to slow down technology, I just want companies to do a better job of rolling out new technology. If consumers gobble up a product when it hits the market, companies will release it, even if it isn't ready or as ready as it should be.

As consumers, we need to calm down and let these manufacturers know we are more conscious of our purchasing decisions. This can probably be another book, but if I planted a seed in your head, I would be happy for now. The generations coming of age today, rarely hear the term "delayed gratification", which previous generations heard constantly.

It does not help our cause if we continue to line up for two days when the new iPhone is released and spend thousands of dollars to replace a device that is still working fine. As much as I enjoy capitalism, we should understand that businesses in a free-market economy will never help us do anything except spend our money.

What does this "buy-it-now" mentality have to do with threatening our privacy and risking our personal information? Well, for one, the methods that people use today to infiltrate our privacy are astounding. I used to have to learn about some new hacking concern once or twice a year. Now, every month or two, I am learning an unfamiliar word for some form of attack that makes me shake my head.

The vectors, or avenues of attack, have become seemingly infinite.

The good old days of spam were a headache indeed, but the only financial loss was in productivity. Advancements in technology have enabled phishing with a 'PH', pronounced like fishing with an 'F', to proliferate and there are now over a dozen specific types of phishing.

Phishing

The electronic theft of information through deceit.

People pretend to be someone else in order to trick a person into handing over information. When phishing started in the 1990's nobody had a name for what they were doing.

The last twenty years have seen us go from not having a name for these online attacks to having so many names that it's hard to keep track of them all. You should be aware of some of the most common phishing attacks so that when something raises a red flag, it makes you think back to this list.

Awareness is the key to prevention.

1. **Vishing**

Phishing using a phone, or voice.

2. **Smishing**

Phishing using texts (or SMS messages).

3. **Search engine phishing**

This uses fake webpages to land you in trouble.

4. **Spear Phishing**

Where normal phishing uses millions of generic emails, this is more targeted to a group or single user. Think of it instead of casting a net, this uses a fishing rod or spear gun.

5. **Whaling**

A term describing a spear phishing attack on a single wealthy or powerful individual.

6. **Pig Butchering**

A long-term investment scam where romantic social media profiles convince victims to slowly invest in crypto schemes or some similar scam.

We also have the relatively new threat of cryptography in an attack called a crypto virus. An attacker tries to get you to open a file that will put a lock on all your files. It ultimately encrypts everything you own so it can't be opened without a password. But, instead of you selecting some crazy long password, the attacker chooses it. This attack is called ransomware because attackers hold the key (the password) hostage and demand a ransom from you.

At the end of this chapter, we will discuss the simplest and most fool-proof protection from these attacks. Keep in mind that the people finding ways around security have much more money supporting them than the security solutions that are available.

TTT – RANSOMWARE PAYOUTS

In 2023, organizations paid out a record $1.1 billion to ransomware attackers.[56]

---

[56] 2023 Ransomware Payouts
http://footnote56.dbtwl.com

This **Chain Analysis** study can be found online as well if you go to our website at **www.DBTWL.com**.[57]

Technology has allowed bad people to prey on society in so many new ways that it is hard to keep track. There has always been theft and there always will be theft, but there has been a steady progression in these attacks from the annoyance of spam to viruses designed for vandalism and interruptions of services.

Then the destructive phase arrived, with the goal of the attack being to simply break stuff.

There was little money in destroying data so the online criminals began stealing data.

Let's divert our attention to Hollywood for a moment...

If you haven't seen the 2024 Jason Statham movie, *The Beekeeper*[58], I would highly recommend it. My wife loves Jason Statham, so convincing her to see it in theaters was effortless. In the movie, an elderly woman that Jason's character was fond of, had her bank accounts drained in a popular online attack.

In a plot twist that surprised nobody, Jason Statham sought justice by hurting people and blowing things up.

In one of the early scenes, Jason Statham uses one of my favorite movie lines when discussing her death. In summary, he states that hurting the elderly is as bad as hurting children, maybe worse.

I have nine children, I never believed that anyone was worse than someone who hurt children, but this line made me reconsider my position. If someone hurt my mother or father-in-law, would I even know about it? Jason Statham has never made me get introspective.

---

[57] the 2024 Crypto Crime Report
http://footnote57.dbtwl.com
[58] The Beekeeper
http://footnote58.dbtwl.com

That is not what he does. In The Beekeeper, he showed me another side. I felt horrible for him losing this woman who meant so much.

Another thing that I decided after seeing this movie, was that I would dedicate more time and resources to helping the elderly avoid being victimized by these online criminals. With that in mind, I try to schedule a free presentation for a senior group for every paid presentation or speech that I do.

I am also planning to give out free e-books to all seniors. I do not want to see a senior victimized because they could not afford a copy of my book. I want this knowledge to be freely available to those most vulnerable in our society.

They will still have to purchase a paperback if that is what they want. My altruism only goes so far. I still have a lot of mouths to feed. I will also be releasing this book in a Large Print edition.

The theft of data became the focus for a brief time and then we moved to blackmail, which is why the world is talking about ransomware and crypto viruses so much today.

Ransomware goals have progressed from getting you to pay to get your data back, to getting you to pay to keep your data private. London Drugs, did not pay a ransom demand in April of 2024 and now hundreds of gigabytes of data from their network has been shared online.[59]

---

[59] London Drugs
http://footnote59.dbtwl.com

TTT – LARGEST RANSOMWARE ATTACKS

Ransomware **attacks** in 2021 **ha**d an **aver**age **pay**out of $570,000 per **att**ack. **T**he **aver**age **co**st of **recover**ing from **a ransom**ware **att**ack is $1.85 **million**. **T**he **largest recor**ded **payout** so far **w**as $40 **million** by CNA **Finan**cial.[60]

Just **t**wo **year**s **later**, **t**he **aver**age **ran**som in 2023 **was** $1.54 **million**. **Accor**ding **t**o **t**he **Sophos** 2023 **Ransom**ware **Repo**rt, **on**ly 70% **of companies attac**ked **had effec**tive **backups** and 46% **paid ran**som **deman**ds.[61]

An **impor**tant **statistic t**o **pon**der **on, is this...** The **aver**age **ou**tage for **a comp**any is 21 **day**s (**up fr**om 16 **days** in 2019). **If y**our **comp**any **ha**d **n**o **compu**ters or data for 21 **days**, how **woul**d **th**ey be **affec**ted? **If a business's** IT **depar**tment **reque**sted a 21-**day business shut**down **t**o **upgr**ade **sy**stems, **we woul**d **n**ot **get happy appro**vals?

Trust me when I say that **th**ey **woul**d **n**ot **react kin**dly.

I have **seen estim**ates **th**at **up t**o 40% **of companies never recover** from **a ransom**ware **att**ack and are **out** of **business** in 6 **mon**ths.

STORY TIME – SMP HEALTH CLOSURE

A ransomware **att**ack **h**it **St. Margaret's Health** in 2021. **SMP Health, t**he **parent organi**zation **of St. Margaret's Health, repor**ted **th**at **th**ey **were down for over** 14 **wee**ks **with n**o **ability t**o **submit claims t**o **insu**rers, **Medi**care, **or Medi**caid.

---

[60] Software One: Ten Key Facts About Ransomware
http://footnote60.dbtwl.com
[61] The State of Ransomware 2023 Infographic – Sophos
http://footnote61.dbtwl.com

In June 2023, St. Mary's Health shut down, closing the only medical facility in Spring Valley, Illinois. The ransomware attack wasn't the only problem they faced, but it was significant and definitely a contributing factor to their closure. [62]

Many large municipalities have suffered as ransomware has become a $10 billion a year industry. Jackson County, Georgia paid $400,000 to unlock files. Lake City, Florida paid $500,000. Riviera Beach, Florida paid $600,000. [63]

The sudden encryption of their 153 web servers forced South Korea web hosting provider, Nayana, to pay $1,000,000 to unlock 3400 websites.

THE PERSONAL TOUCH

This book suddenly took a dark turn down a path of corporate assault, but what does all this have to do with you?

The title of this book, <u>Don't Be the Weakest Link: How to Protect Your Personal Information in a Digital World</u>, was basically chosen for this example. Seeing those payouts is just the surface because most companies do not want the government, public, or shareholders to know that they paid a ransom of any amount. It highlights critical flaws in business operations which affect customer confidence and share prices. I have had to recover from ransomware on four occasions and every single time there was one thing in common. We ignored the ransom demand.

---

[62] SMP Health story
http://footnote62.dbtwl.com
[63] Municipalities Hit Hard with Ransomware
http://footnote63.dbtwl.com

We found the infiltration point, whether it was technology or a person, and we fixed it. We then restored all our data from backups and carried on. In one instance, we were down less than 48 hours.

Did you catch on to your part there? Where were you involved in the complete disaster recovery? According to some estimates, over 65% of ransomware attacks are results of phishing attacks. The lowest estimate I have seen was 13% from Sophos.[64]

We, as technology users, must make a concerted effort to be better at protecting ourselves. If you are not an accountant, you should not be opening an email with a subject line, "here is your final invoice."

If you are an accountant, I want to say how much I apologize that technology has allowed you to be the focal point of so many attacks. Stopping these incidents will rely on educating people with computers, cell phones, and email accounts and that is a lot of people.

> Accountants have access to money and are the targets of numerous phishing attacks.

BLACKMAIL

As an IT Professional, I always recommend that clients do not consider paying a ransom, but this advice is not always in the best interest of the company, its shareholders, employees, or customers.

My recommendation is to always tell them to pound sand. We clean infected devices, restore our data from backups, and start rebuilding, hoping we suffered insignificant data loss. There are few downsides to ignoring the ransomware demand, unless I didn't do my job right and the backups are not available for some reason.

---

[64] The State of Ransomware 2023 – Sophos
http://footnote64.dbtwl.com

Paying a ransom however, has many downsides. It rewards a criminal enterprise for starters. Paying does not guarantee that your data will be unlocked. It also does not mean that you are done paying. A Proofpoint study (2024 State of the Phish) claims that 59% of companies that pay a ransom are forced to pay a second ransom. Of that 59%, 15% refused a second payment and 1% paid two ransoms and still never saw their data.[65]

I mentioned that there are few downsides to not paying, but the big one is if the criminals gained access to your data. Encrypting it is bad for you, but having it stolen, and then encrypted, can be much more significant.

Without paying the ransom, your data is most likely going to be shared online with anyone who wants to see it or possibly pay for it. This may happen regardless of whether you paid the ransom.

You can probably understand why a company may choose to ignore my advice and pay a ransom just for a chance to keep some confidential data out of the public eye. When confidential designs of Apple iPhone components were compromised through one of their third-party vendors, Apple did not hesitate to pay to keep their secrets from spreading far and wide.

STORY TIME – GRANT MCEWAN UNIVERSITY

In 2017, one of Alberta's largest universities was the victim of a Spear Phishing attack that netted the fraudsters almost $12M. The police froze $11.4M out of the $11.8M paid out, preventing it from being lost, but $400,000 will probably never be recovered.[66] This is ignoring legal costs to regain the funds from three different continents.

---

[65] 2024 State of the Phish – Proofpoint
http://footnote65.dbtwl.com
[66] Grant McEwan University $11.8M loss
http://footnote66.dbtwl.com

The finance department received an email from a construction client that they needed to change the bank account for the deposits. The email address, signature, and website all looked correct. The person who emailed the school certainly looked legit and at the end of the day, the signature looked right and had the construction company's logo, so the school suspected nothing.

They saw no red flags. Keep reading for more details on red flags.

But finance departments need to be extremely wary, and employees of these departments need specialized training. No account should ever be changed without corroboration with a phone call and follow-up email making sure that the corroborating phone call was documented in writing. And never make the phone call with the number in the email's signature. Always assume that the account has been compromised and look the number up from your previously saved contact list.

As a last resort, look up the contact information on their website.

WHAT'S THE SOLUTION?

I want to tell you about a near-foolproof solution for never getting in trouble with a crypto virus. It is simply this... be wary. It might not be foolproof, but it is literally the best solution out there, minus avoiding technology altogether.

The fastest way to learn how to be wary is to read this chapter through to the end, or the whole book, until you have a Knowledge Ranking of at least a "B". All the hyperlinks in the footnotes are on the www.DBTWL.com website for your additional reference.

I told you it was simple. From an IT perspective, most attacks are recoverable. We back up data so that when it is encrypted, erased, or infected, we just shut stuff down, delete the compromised data, rebuild what needs rebuilding, and then restore the data from backups. This sounds much simpler than the actual implementation, but the plan is sound and has worked millions of times.

> The best solution to an attack will always be prevention.
> The best way to prevent an attack is with
> your knowledge and your good habits.

When I talk to people during my presentations, I really focus on these phishing attacks louder than I would like to, because I truly believe that people are the weakest link in the security chain. Mostly because many people don't realize what's at stake and because they don't know their options. Therefore, all IT professionals should have a Knowledge Ranking of "A" or "B" moving to an "A" if they are in the beginning of their career.

One of our most sincere goals is to help as many people as possible become an "A" or "B" with their Knowledge Ranking.

RED FLAGS

I have posted several videos on social media and there is a free cut-sheet on our website (**www.DBTWL.com/cut-sheets**) that you can download called "Raise a Red Flag". [67]

If you get an email that says you need to pay an overdue invoice, but your invoices are usually different in any way, a red flag should go up. Once that red flag is flying in the wind, manage that email with the consideration that you could be the reason that your company is shut down for 21 days.

---

[67] DBTWL Cut-Sheets
http://footnote67.dbtwl.com

Keep in mind that the goal of the attack on you might not be to get your money, but to get you to help steal someone else's money.

In a recent intrusion I was dealing with, we assumed the police were racing to prevent money from leaving the country, but the criminals were using the proceeds of a hack in Canada to pay unwitting victims of other attacks with the profits from this attack. They were using other victims to launder their money.

As an IT professional, I feel horrible for you if you are an executive or an accountant because most current phishing attacks are aimed at you for a few reasons... you control the money, and you have access to a lot of corporate systems and data. Accounting and administrative data is valuable and if it is not restorable, it is more likely that a ransom demand will be paid in hopes of retrieving it.

IT staff are often targets because we are administrators on the network and an attack from our computer causes the most harm, but we never sign away money. We have no access to any finances.

Accountants are the best of both worlds, and what accountant isn't intrigued by an email that says, "FINAL NOTICE... pay this invoice today... OVERDUE... URGENT."

And that brings us to our first Red Flag!

Red Flag #1

Always be wary of any subject line in all capital letters. As a matter of fact, let's assume that anything in capital letters should raise a red flag.

Capital letters are like yelling in text. Do you reply to people who are yelling at you?

Red Flag #2

Emails with links or attachments should always be suspect.

It is a best practice to email, text, or phone the person who sent the email to confirm that they meant to send you the link or attachment. If the email was sent as part of a virus payload, then the owner of the email will have no idea about it.

Red Flag #3

Now we have to talk about spelling and grammar if we are going to discuss hackers, spammers, and their email correspondence. In 2020 I started planning to remove this 'red flag' from my presentations. With every new technology or update, I thought I was one step closer and I have been waiting for these criminal masterminds to start adopting the tools we use in our daily life. I am still waiting.

For some reason, these people who send the phishing emails have failed to figure out how to use spell check, Grammarly, pro-writing aid, ChatGPT, or dictionaries.

If you see a glaring mistake in spelling, grammar, or punctuation, the red flags should be popping up.

If you ever suspect that someone's email was hacked, do not reply to the email as it may go right back to the person who hacked it. Send them a new email from your saved contact or phone them directly, and not from the phone number in the email's signature. If you haven't dealt with the company before or don't have their contact info saved, open a web browser and do a search for the company contact info.

If the email address is valid, you can now have a conversation. It probably won't take long before you will realize that the person who emailed did not grow up speaking English. You might get a simple response explaining that the invoice was for a valid order that someone forgot to mention but you might just get a pile of red flags.

Don't worry about that "English" comment sounding racist or xenophobic, it is not. It is a simple fact that you can use to help you save your company or your family from learning a painful lesson. Few hackers are based in Canada or the USA (or choose your Western nation... UK, Australia, etc.).

Hackers really want to avoid Western nations where law enforcement agencies work together. The punishment in these nations is usually swift and significant. Turkey and Malaysia, not so much. China, Russia, and North Korea, not at all.

Red Flag #4

Watch the subject lines of the emails. Watch for capital letters and errors, but also look for inconsistences with your role. If you aren't in accounting, you should never open an email about invoices. If you are receiving an email about a subject that typically isn't part of your job, this should raise a red flag.

Red Flag #5

This is the To and From box. First, make sure that the email is addressed to you. I have an email for my company that starts with shayne@ but I also have alias accounts like shayne.kawalilak@. If the email was addressed to my full name, that raises a red flag because I do not share that address with anyone.

In my presentations, I use an example of an email that I received from Diaz Keaton about an office supply order I supposedly made. Was Diaz's email address diaz@ or dkeaton@ or even accounting@?

Nope.

Diaz Keaton's email was **rofedyviruxidi**@vocalriyaz.com. There are people in Finland that could not read that email. How on earth does that make any sense? This is a huge red flag.

Red Flag #6

The last red flag is all about time. It should raise a red flag if the email is all about the urgency. Is something past due or is this a final notice? If you don't get these all the time, this should raise a red flag.

The email will also have a sent time. If you aren't used to getting emails after hours and this one was sent at 1am or on a Saturday, this should be a red flag for you.

If you aren't sure about an email's validity, forward the email to your IT department. If you don't have an IT department, forward it to a friend who works in IT or knows much more about technology. If you really don't know anyone who knows more about this than you, or you get so many of these that it is too bothersome to send them all, send it to your boss and suggest that you need access to a geek to help with the red flags.

THE SIN OF IT DEPARTMENTS

We have to step back for a minute to talk about one of the most prevalent security issues today and why IT Departments around the world are promoting such a security threat. The risk comes from that automated password rest policy that we spoke about earlier in **Chapter 2: Passwords are Stupid**.

If you have ever received an email saying that your password was expiring, then the person who is in control of your email simply doesn't understand or doesn't care about your security. In the vast majority of situations, the people in charge of the IT policies simply are not aware of how insecure this policy is. I used to say all of them but I have met some people who simply refuse to believe that their actions are causing so much harm.

The fact is simple, and I have been saying this since 2002, forcing people to reset their password on a schedule is insecure. Many reasons were discussed already but now I need you to start watching for red flags and this is a huge one.

There are a few websites to change a Microsoft password (aside from corporate redirections) and they are microsoftonline.com, office.com, live.com, and microsoft.com but there are over 10,000 websites that look exactly like a Microsoft login page. These pages are run by criminals.

When my clients get an email saying that their password has expired, they are shocked. Red flags are popping up all over because they have never seen that email before.

If you received that email four or five times a year for the past 10 years, there would be no red flag. You would not be suspicious at all because your IT department had programmed you to expect those emails.

I tell people if they ever see these things to NEVER go to the link to reset their password, always go to microsoft.com and find a login link to reset their password. If it is an email account which I manage, I welcome them to forward the email to me and ask for an explanation. I will determine what happened and apologize if it was my fault. Typically, a short look reveals the email as a scam.

If you have a 'great' passphrase already, and you are using MFA, preferably NOT via text, then I want you to keep the old password unless you think there is any reason to believe that it has been compromised in any way.

If someone in your IT department does not agree with me, invite them to contact me. I would be more than happy to defend my position because I have never heard a plausible argument against it.

One of the first people that I ever heard agree with me was Kevin Mitnick. He stated the same thing in his book, <u>The Art of Invisibility</u>. That book was released in 2019 and Kevin Mitnick, one of the most famous hackers-turned-security-gurus, was only the second or third person I had ever met who agreed with me.

I mentioned earlier that Microsoft finally started agreeing with me (and Kevin) in 2022. On October 12, 2022, Microsoft released a short article on their website titled, "Set the password expiration policy for your organization". In most ways, it was a simple how-to post except, in that article, Microsoft stated, "current research strongly indicates that mandated password changes do more harm than good".[68]

I was in shock. I felt so vindicated after so many years of taking the sneers. Somehow, I still meet IT professionals today, who disagree with me after my presentations or during our planning meetings beforehand.

I have several various presentations that focus on different topics all geared toward protecting your data. Each one of them thoroughly discusses this chapter. I usually talk about MFA, but not always. I often mention anti-virus and malware. Frequently I discuss hacking.

I always talk about phishing. Every single time I have spoken I cover this topic without fail. I recommend you read this chapter again when you finish this book (or read the whole book again) so that you are more aware of the dangers and the methods that these villains use so that you see the red flags more often.

EMAIL SPOOFING

We need to take a moment to talk about email spoofing.

---

[68] Microsoft Password Expiration Policy
http://footnote68.dbtwl.com

This is emailing from an account that looks like it is from someone other than the actual sender. The most important thing for you to understand about email spoofing is that it is possible.

Just because you receive an email from your boss, your brother, or your best friend, it does not mean that they truly sent that email. If I received an email from a good friend, let's call him Charles, saying he was in Asia visiting his brother and he needed $5000, I would immediately text or phone him. I would not reply to the email for verification because I value my money.

I want verification because I assume that someone has access to his email account, so I want to see if they have his phone as well, or if he's truly in trouble. If he texts back that he legitimately needs the money, even though my Response Ranking is a 4, I am still skeptical. Unless this friend calls and asks you for money all the time, you should be skeptical too.

Charles has never asked me for money. Red Flag!

With the amazing advancements in A.I. technology, I don't know that I trust hearing his voice blindly either.

My skeptical brain is now checking with his wife. Did he even travel halfway around the world without letting me know? This may sound a little crazy, but I don't have $5000 that I don't have something better to do with than donating it to a criminal from Thailand or Malaysia. I own a boat!

It's not crazy to check and double check, especially since Charles has never asked to borrow money before. It immediately raised the red flag we talked about earlier.

In our example, he has emailed me a request, and now returned a text. I could transfer that money to him, but I'm not sure I am that gullible of an A4. I am aware and informed, so I am assuming now that someone found his phone unlocked and has access to his texts and his email on that device.

Remember that a 2 and a 4 on the Weakest Link Scale can both have exactly the same level of education and skills regarding technology, but they respond differently. When I go to Disneyland, everyone knows as I posted to social media (this is not a good habit), I have out of office auto responders on my email, and I probably blog about it. If you didn't know where I was for the whole two weeks, then you simply didn't care, or you weren't paying attention.

Charles has a Response Ranking of 2 with the same knowledge as me. Even though we know about the same threats, he absolutely behaves differently toward them. Although Charles has never sent me an email requesting any money, he has absolutely returned from a trip to Asia that I did not know he went on until he returned.

His personal information is less likely to be compromised because even if someone hacked his email, reading his emails would barely give them a clue that he was traveling.

If hackers somehow found out that he was in Asia and sent all his friends an email asking for money, the hackers would deal with many people with red flags because only a few of them knew he was in Asia to start with. That is another huge reason that a person with a Response Ranking of 2 is more secure than one with a 4.

A Response Ranking of 2 means you are, by nature,
a more cautious and private individual.

EMAIL HACKING

While editing this chapter, in my professional life, I am assisting a client who experienced a compromise and lost almost $200,000 to a calculated spear phishing attack. Let's call the victim Mr. O. for now. Well, Mr. O. had one of his email accounts hacked and those hackers requested bank account changes to the companies that they work with. Some of those companies changed the account that they paid Mr. O's company with.

We recently had to deal with a serious hacking issue with a couple of friends from the lake where we spend all our spare time in the summer. Let's call them Dustin and Sandra, just for the heck of it. I received a call early in the morning and they were understandably freaking out because their customers were calling them to say that they were receiving emails asking for money.

Someone had infiltrated their company email account and been sending out these email requests. This is a dreadful position for a small business, but one that happens all too often.

I want to divert this commentary quickly just to give a little guidance. If your email is hacked, call a professional geek for help as soon as possible. You need to regain control of the email account immediately and then communicate the breach to your customers, even before the police.

Police can do an investigation after the fact, and they might regain financial losses, but your best chance of getting money back is to contact the clients who received emails from the hackers and help them correct any banking changes the hackers might have already made.

One of these problems was that these friends were using "free" email services that have fewer management features and less security and the other hack was because of users not implementing security features like MFA with email systems.

If you own a company, buy a domain name for $20 per year, pay $10 per month for a professional email service, and invest $200 on a professional geek to set it up for you. Having this done right the first time doesn't just look professional but can save you a lot of stress or money down the road.

Back to these hackers…

You may get an email trying to blackmail you, but they will rarely have anything worth blackmailing you over. Millions of people have received an email from an unknown person saying that they have hacked something and stolen information, browsing history, or taken pictures with their webcam. Send them money or the info goes public.

Senders of these emails typically provide no supporting information. They have your email and IP address or home address. That's it. Do you remember that list of information about you that might be available on the internet way back in **Chapter 1: Find Your Weakness**? Most of the time, the lack of evidence means they are trying to hustle you by showing off some information that impresses most people.

You are already more knowledgeable than "most" people.

But sometimes, the threat is real.

STORY TIME – CASSIDY WOLF

In 2013, authorities arrested a foolish 19-year-old kid named Jared (you can look him up, but I don't want to make this kid more famous). He was arrested for computer hacking and blackmail. Nobody should know his name and he should have served his 18 months in prison without being a footnote.

He stole webcam videos of people who didn't know their cameras were compromised, but he only gained notoriety because he took some of those videos with the webcam of Cassidy Wolf, Miss Teen USA 2013.

Jared hacked over 100 cameras and blackmailed dozens of women, but young Cassidy Wolf was having none of that. She went to the media and called him out. The FBI arrested him, and the rest is history.[69]

We will speak more about your webcams in **Chapter 11: Hitting Closer to Home**.

---

[69] Cassidy Wolf – Miss Teen USA
http://footnote69.dbtwl.com

PLAY ALONG

Task 8-1 Back-Up Your Personal Data

I would like you to get a USB drive or something that isn't always connected to your computer and I would like you to copy all your documents and family photos to it. Just in case. This is your rainy-day backup.

There is a computer geek who gets paid a lot of money to ensure that data at your workplace is backed up and secure, and I simply want to make sure that you implement the same practices to some extent in your home life.

Task 8-2 Watch a Couple Short Videos

The second task I will also ask of you is a little more fun and educational.

Open your web browser and go to www.DBTWL.com or www.DontBeTheWeakestLink.com click on The Book > Chapter 8 > Play Along.

In here you will see examples of phishing attempts as well as educational and humorous videos relating to this chapter. If you only watch one video, watch the one from "Justified". That one makes me smile all day long and not just because I relish most of Timothy Olyphant's work.

_____

_____

_____

CHAPTER 9: SMOOTH CRIMINALS

Up to this point, our discussion has revolved around what hackers take from you, specifically data. We have talked about some of their goals in spreading viruses, and we have talked about blackmail. We haven't talked so much about corporate espionage because that is not a typical worry for the target audience of this book.

I will tell you, though, that corporate data loss is the reason that I do most of my presentations. Companies know that if they help their employees move up in the Knowledge Ranking, making them better stewards of their personal information, they will use that knowledge in securing the corporate data they are entrusted with.

It needs to be clear to you why a hacker would prefer access to your company's data instead of yours. Your computer might have your credit card information, but your company's server might have the credit info of millions of users. Your computer might have a secret recipe from your grandmother, but your company might have the Colonel's recipe with those eleven herbs and spices. It doesn't take a rocket scientist to see where the money is.

They may also just have a vulnerable server with a connection to the internet that is 100 times faster than anything you have at home. Consider if your company has a monstrous server with an extremely fast connection to the internet and then think about something that you did, or failed to do, that gave a hacker access to that server.

They can then use that server to spread viruses, hack other companies, hack into government agencies, or just mine for crypto currency at your company's expense. You might not even find out about the compromise before the police start knocking on your door.

A report released in February 2024, pointing out government espionage that allowed Chinese government actors to infiltrate key infrastructure networks in energy, transportation, communication, as well as wastewater and waste sectors. [70] The key part of this report is the claim that foreign hackers were stealthily sitting in American sites for up to five years just waiting for someone to say "go".

This report was co-authored by American organizations like CISA (**Cybersecurity & Infrastructure Security Agency**), the NSA (**National Security Agency**), the FBI (**Federal Bureau of Investigation**), the TSA (**Transportation Security Administration**), the EPA (**Environmental Protection Agency**), and the **Department of Energy**.

---

[70] PRC Hacker Report
http://footnote70.dbtwl.com

Other co-authors of the study include foreign organizations like the Australian Cyber Security Centre, New Zealand's National Cyber Security Centre, Britain's National Cyber Security Centre, and the Canadian Centre of Cyber Security. You can see that this report has some heavy hitters behind it. Granted, some people have accused some of these organizations of spreading as much propaganda as facts, but in this area of reporting, I tend to trust the broad strokes intently.

IT'S TIME TO SCARE YOU

Our primary goal is to share the knowledge to move everyone up a few notches on the Knowledge Ranking. If you recall when we discussed the Weakest Link Scale, remember Charles and I were both A's on the Knowledge Ranking even though we were a 2 and 4 on the Response Ranking. Despite our knowledge being the same, we respond much differently to threats.

We want you to gain the knowledge that will help you avoid being one of those people sitting in a boardroom, explaining why your actions have cost the company millions of dollars.

The best hackers aren't famous. Nobody knows who they are because they compromise systems, take what they want, and disappear before anyone knows they are there. What could be scarier than a hacker you thought of as a ghost?

Let's discuss the most significant threat to personal security that exists. Pay attention here and consider all the things we have discussed that aim against you in your mission to protect your personal data.

We have talked about:

1. **Personal data theft,**
2. **Creating great passwords,**
3. using **passphrases instead of passwords,**
4. **implem**enting **password mana**gers,
5. how to use **browsers** and **search engines** more **safely,**
6. **implem**enting MFA or **Multi-Fac**tor **Authent**ication,
7. an**ti-vir**us and an**ti-malw**are **effecti**veness, and
8. **ranso**mware.

We've **hopef**ully **taught** you a few **things** that **will help prevent hack**ers from **taking** your **money** or your job, but **this** is **going** to be a much more **significant** topic. Now we are **going** to **talk about** someone **taking some**thing from you that you can't so **easily replace** as your **life savi**ngs.

We're **going** to **talk about** losing **your**self, your **iden**tity.

We have all heard about identity theft, but more and more people are being affected by it, and for some reason, we still treat it like a disease and assume it will only happen to others. The difference between some diseases and identity theft is that we know what causes identity theft and we know how to reduce the threat. What we need is for more people to educate themselves like you are doing right now (so give this book away when you are done, or buy a copy for a friend).

We, as a tech community, need to spread this knowledge until it is so difficult to steal someone's identity that it simply isn't worth trying. We need to turn you from an easy victim to an individual that makes criminals turn away.

TTT – IDENTITY THEFT BY THE NUMBERS

In 2023, over 1.4 million **Americans** were victims of identity theft. **Experts predict** that **identity theft protection services will become a** $28 **billion indus**try by 2029, **highli**ghting the **magni**tude of the issue.

Annual identity theft cases have over tripled since 2017 according to identitytheft.org.[71]

If you do everything else in this book to protect your personal information, there are still some extra things you should pursue to protect yourself from identity theft and here are some action steps...

1. Check your credit report often.

This is a simple step that can save you a tremendous headache down the road. Your credit report will show you every credit account you have, or have had, and show your balances. If you are making payments on a car that you didn't purchase and you've never driven, it will show up here, hopefully raising a big red flag.

Understand the difficulty of tracking your credit if someone else has a credit card in your name with a different address. They're making monthly payments, and everything is going great... until they stop. Then things will not go so well for you.

2. Get rid of paper.

Paper is the launching point of many identity theft attacks because so much personal information is printed on paper. Having all your bills come to your email or only exist on a website makes it much easier to secure than a piece of paper that blew out a car window, was accidentally recycled, or thrown out with the trash. When you have paper, make sure you keep it safe.

Treat documents with account numbers and personal information like piles of cash. Do not leave them lying around. Do not let them fall in the garbage or recycling or get misplaced. Be sure that you shred all this paper when you're done with it.

---

[71] IdentityTheft.org
http://footnote71.dbtwl.com

When cleaning off your desk or a filing cabinet, do not throw away anything without looking at it carefully. If you have any doubt about the personal information, shred it.

> If in doubt, shred on the side of caution.

3. Use a credit card instead of a debit card.

Credit card companies have been dealing with theft for decades and most countries have laws in place to protect consumers from online fraud and identity theft, but bank debit cards don't always enjoy the same protection. In the USA the Fair Credit Billing Act protects you from credit card fraud. Most countries have similar protections in their legal system.

For the same reason, I do not recommend buying something from someone with any form of bank transfer or crypto currency unless you have done so in the past or truly trust that the online purchase will be sent to you.

4. Review. Review. Review.

I can't say this enough in my personal life and my business life. Reviewing monthly statements is a simple task that will help you ensure that all your purchases were yours. This painless action can save you a great deal of trouble and money. You may find purchases that a family member made, that you forgot about, but you may also find the earliest evidence of criminal activity, and this is the fastest way to stop it dead in its tracks.

5. There is no such thing as secure Wi-Fi.

While the chances of your home Wi-Fi being hacked are slim, you should never trust free Wi-Fi from a local coffee shop, store at the mall, or hotel. Just being on these inherently insecure networks, and just by logging on to free Wi-Fi, you are giving away access to your computer or phone. Any child with a piece of software running on a laptop can view your traffic. This does not take sophisticated equipment or decades of education or experience.

Charles and I both understand security and encryption of wireless networks. Neither of us use public Wi-Fi but if we ever had to, we would never log into an account for a bank or a credit card. The only reason I could ever see using public Wi-Fi is that if there was no cell coverage and I needed an online video to keep a child happy.

More times than not though, I avoid public Wi-Fi completely and hotspot from my cell phone.

Cell phones are just getting so inexpensive, and their available data usage is so high that the public wireless makes less and less sense. I'd love to tell you that Charles never uses public Wi-Fi because he is a 2. Being a 2 on the Response Ranking doesn't make it impossible to use public Wi-Fi but it makes it much less likely to happen. Charles and I agree closely on public Wi-Fi usage.

Charles has made a specific habit that I have recently adopted. When he creates a connection to a Wi-Fi network, whether it's a hotel or any public place, he specifically goes into that connection to make sure that his wireless never connects automatically. This is a simple habit to form and quite smart. I don't know why I wasn't doing it already.

This week I visited a hotel that I haven't been to in over a year. It was no surprise to me that my laptop logged into the Wi-Fi automatically when I turned it on.

I immediately turned off the automatic connection and added a note to include Charles's advice in this book.

Charles and I also make a habit of turning our Wi-Fi off on our phone when we are not specifically using it. Leaving Wi-Fi enabled constantly allows hackers to see what networks your phone or laptop is searching for, giving them a major opportunity to cause you harm.

It's more effort, but it is a positive step in taking your security to a new level.

STORY TIME – 23 AND ME

There are undoubtedly better stories about corporate espionage, but since we are going to talk more about the personal losses you might suffer from a hack, I don't think we could get more personal than discussing the 2023 hack of 23andMe.[72]

23andMe is a private company that provides customers with genetic testing services for a little spit and a small fee. The lure of finding out what your DNA says about your ancestry and predisposition to medical subjects is appealing, to say the least.

There was a time when I was considering this exact thing as I've never met my father, and I thought it would be nice to know more about my medical proclivities. This wasn't 30 years ago, but this was in 2021, well into my writing of this book. My Knowledge Ranking was already up at the top of the scale, but curiosity and desire sometimes bypass all the Red Flags and allows us to do things that we might otherwise never consider, especially if we have a Response Rank of 4 or 5.

Thankfully, I had Charles. We were going through the drafting of the book chapter by chapter so I could get his input and when I mentioned that I was considering sending my DNA in, he laughed. He thought I was making a joke for the book.

Needless to say, it only took him a few minutes to wake me up out of my cloudy thoughts.

---

[72] 23andMe Hack
http://footnote72.dbtwl.com

If your **Response Rank** is a 1 or a 2, like **Charles**, giving your DNA to any company just sounds absurd. If your **Knowledge Ranking** is a **D** or **F**, you might not be aware of the risk.

If your **Knowledge Rank** is a **D** or your **Response Rank** is a 4, giving away your DNA is a much more likely situation. My A4 brain makes me hesitant but without **Charles** to bounce ideas off, I might have signed up.

Alas, neither **Charles** nor I have ever done anything like this. Apparently, this is a good thing.

Hackers targeted and breached 23andMe's security system in October 2023. The company claims it was because of a credential stuffing attack. If you recall from <u>Chapter 2: Passwords are Stupid</u>, this attack exists where people use the same password for different services or accounts. I can't believe that anyone would use the same password for their diet-tracking website and their 23andMe corporate login, but stranger things have happened.

This was not a random employee. This was a user with an administrative account that was re-using another password on their corporate login. We are likely discussing another geek or upper manager. I deliberately do not use "IT professional" here for good reason.

In what I believe may become one of the most significant hacks in human history to this date, over 7 million customers had unknown amounts of their DNA records stolen. In the future, someone might use that data to clone you in a literal sense.

This takes identity theft to a whole new level.

If I were a betting man, I would not be counting on the survival of 23andMe as a company and definitely wouldn't want to depend on it as a primary source of income.

In another related story, Atlas Biomed, a DNA testing company with offices in the UK, has seemingly shut down. Nobody is sure where they went or when they closed their doors but when their website went down, customers started asking questions. [73]

This company was probably never hacked, but an unknown number of people now have no idea where their DNA information has gone or what it might be used for in the future. The BBC seems to think that the only remaining link to the company is a Moscow address for a Russian Billionaire.

This does not bode well for their customers.

IDENTITY THEFT

For the rest of this chapter, let's assume that there is only one copy of you.

What exactly is identity theft and what could realistically happen to you if someone found some of your information? Using your identity by another individual without your consent could cause damage that can range from someone charging a new Shawn Mendes song to your credit card to you ending up in prison. This is quite a varied range.

I suppose at the extreme, it could be worse. Nobody wants to live Angela Bennett's life from *The Net.* [74]

If you haven't seen *The Net,* with Sandra Bullock, then you likely don't understand how bad identity theft can be. In the movie, a dark organization replaced Sandra Bullock's character with one of their people when she went on vacation. During that vacation, they tried to kill her.

---

[73] Atlas Biomed
http://footnote73.dbtwl.com
[74] Movie – The Net
http://footnote74.dbtwl.com

I am not saying this is likely or even probable, but I would also be shocked if it hadn't happened in real life... more than once.

What I can tell you, from a technological perspective, is that this scenario is 100% possible. There are many other objectives to an identity thief that are less significant than the complete destruction of your life. You don't want to be a victim to any of them.

Many times, identity thieves don't intend to hurt a victim at all. Often, they just want to use a name and credit card to live their life. The problem comes when they decide to start over with someone else's identity. That new identity will come with a new credit rating and suddenly it makes sense to stop paying those bills that were in your name.

A. Your hidden career

Imagine filing your income tax and finding out that, while you were working 40 hours a week last year at your accounting job in California, you were also a full-time employee at a large poultry farm in Indiana. I imagine this might push you into a new tax bracket. Wouldn't that reassessment come as a surprise?

People who enter the United States illegally can't get legal full-time jobs or get social security numbers (this is changing in some states), but they can easily use yours with prospective employers. Employers need to tell the IRS who they paid all year. How important do you think it is that they know the worker's real name? Not very in some cases, especially for seasonal workers.

That Social Security Number is often used to rent property because people with bad credit can have a difficult time renting an apartment. Your number allows them to pass a credit check. These people are often in the same city as you and get your information from stolen mail or vehicles.

Please stop here and think about your belongings and remember
that cash might not be the primary target if your purse goes missing
or someone breaks into your car and pulls everything out of the glove
box. The thief might not have much value for your cash or your credit
cards, they may be playing a much longer game… with your personal
identity.

B. Free medical insurance

Think about the last time you went to the hospital for something.
They cared much more about whether you had medical insurance
than if you were sick. Often, if you know your birthday and address,
you can just fill out a form and voila, free healthcare.

It's just like being in Canada, except without the 7-hour wait to
see a doctor.

C. Tax returns

Imagine someone who has been using your identity to live for a
year or more and you don't even know that they're doing it. They go
through your mail one day and see your tax return. Imagine the
problem you will have trying to convince the government that the
endorsement at the bank isn't your signature, and you did not get your
tax return check. Isn't imagination wonderful?

The fact is that criminals can use your name to build-up your
credit and, on some occasions, they spread their life across several
stolen identities. This makes it easy to skip out on one name if they
move without paying a few months' rent. Their car and job are in
different names, so only the name they were using on the rental
application is the one getting the bad credit rating and collection
agency attention.

When a collection agency or credit card company goes searching for you, who do they find? That's right, they find the real you because you aren't the one who has been hiding your address.

The best defense against identity theft is a good offense. Proactively doing the things in this book should see you well on your way to live your life however you please, but in a safer manner. You can be more carefree, with a Response Ranking of 3, 4, or 5, or more protected, like a number 1 or 2. Either way, your knowledge is going to make you a much happier and safer person.

If you want to learn more about protecting your identity or need assistance recovering from identity theft, you can find more resources online at www.DBTWL.com or in the <u>Additional **Reading** List</u> section of this book.

If you just want to understand what it takes to disappear or if you want to try living as a 1, I thoroughly enjoyed *How to Disappear: Erase Your Digital Footprint, Leave False Trails, and Vanish without a Trace* by Frank M Ahearn & Eileen C Horan.

BIGGER THREATS

In 2022, a large amount of evidence came out that the FBI and DOJ in the USA had spent over two years in a partnership with big tech giants, including Facebook, Twitter (now X), and several others. The fact is that these government agencies have been caught censoring the speech that Americans so proudly claim is "free". How difficult is it to imagine that they are still tracking personal information on their citizens?

DOJ: Department of Justice

The federal executive department of the United States government responsible for enforcing federal laws and administering justice.

Not only is this likely, but we believe you can confidently count on it.

Companies using your data to send you ads or selling the information to another company so that they can sell you something is basically what Google, and most social media companies, do as a business. It is doubtful that any of us ever recall checking a box allowing big tech companies to share our information about our social media accounts with the government. I know I didn't.

I checked with Charles and he looked at me funny. I forgot he has no social media accounts. The life of a 2 has so much more free time.

Poor Edward Snowden isn't living a glamorous life in Siberia because that was his choice. He is relaxing in Russia because the US government thought it was treasonous to be an American whistle-blower and tell the public that his employer was tracking phone calls and data on hundreds of millions of American citizens. If he had worked for Google or Facebook, nobody would have been shocked and we would have never remembered his name.

But Edward Snowden did not work for a big-tech firm, he worked for the NSA (the National Security Agency). He is now wanted for treason because he did what any American probably should have done when he found out that his employer was violating a dozen laws.

If you really want to know what could happen if someone could gain access to your personal information, watch the hit TV show, *Person of Interest*[75], starring Jim Caviezel. It stays away from the darker possibilities for the first season, but it shows what is possible with technology.

It is a nightmare for anyone who strives to have a Response Ranking of 1.

---

[75] TV Show - Person of Interest
http://footnote75.dbtwl.com

You have heard me discuss the threats to executives and finance staff due to their roles. There is one more group that gets hammered hard by hackers and that is IT staff. That's right, the people entrusted to protect the network are often the ones at the end of spear phishing attacks where hackers focus a detailed campaign at one or two individuals.

STORY TIME – MGM HACK

In 2023 the MGM Resorts was hacked by a criminal convincing an IT staff member to reset a password for one of the employees.[76] You would think that there would be a reasonable amount of checks and balances for a remote service like this, but in many instances, there are not as many as you would think.

There are FOUR things that I want you to take away from the MGM hack whether you have heard of it before today or not. For the record, I might not have dug into it more closely when it happened except that I stay at an MGM property in Las Vegas at least once or twice a year.

Takeaway 1: The loss of personal info was one of key contributors to the success of the hack. If hackers didn't have any personal info on the person that they were impersonating, there would have been many more red flags with the MGM IT help desk. We will discuss this in many places in this book because it is so important.

Regardless of whether your Response Rank is a 2 like Charles, or a 4 like me, if we have a Knowledge Rank of a C, we should be aware of these threats and know how they can happen. We need to stop sharing as much information as we do.

---

[76] MGM Hack
http://footnote76.dbtwl.com

Takeaway 2: If you heard about the MGM hack you were probably shocked at the magnitude of it. MGM was basically back in the 70's with much of their systems for a week to a month. It wasn't just online reservations or billing systems but think about room service, casino management, parking, and even room locks. Imagine not being able to get into your room for a week without an escort with a master key.

In reality, the hackers wanted money and they thought they could get it by either encrypting all MGM data and being paid for the encryption password. If that failed, and it did, maybe MGM would pay to prevent their stolen data from being released online. MGM did not, and the hackers did.

All of those system shutdowns were part of the MGM resolution strategy trying to contain the hackers in a single system to limit how much data they could steal and encrypt. At the end of the day, it was too little too late.

Takeaway 3: The data that was taken included employee and guest data and I have not heard of a single password to anything being compromised. Employees lost the most, with some reports saying that they lost everything from social security numbers to banking information.

Guests lost names, driver's license info, date of birth, and some even lost their social security number and passport information. My biggest concern is that a previous MGM breach in 2019 included dates of birth, Email addresses, names, phone numbers, and physical addresses. I am included in this group of victims as well.

You might think that the hackers got nothing from the theft but all that raw data is exactly how they breached MGM in the first place. They had the ability to answer enough personal questions about an employee to convince the IT staff that they were that person.

Takeaway 4: While **I would confid**ently say that the data that was **compro**mised from MGM **Resort**s was worth a significant amount to the thieves' future, money is appreciated by these cyber-criminals as well, and a week before MGM was being hacked, Caesars up the strip went through much the same attack but Caesars opted to pay a $15M ransom and barely anyone reported on their breech.

The central theme of this book is to equip you with the knowledge and skills to avoid being the weakest link in data security, even if you are already an IT professional with an A for a Knowledge Rank.

DEEP FAKES

I need to step off the tracks for a moment and warn you about deep fakes. The technology is out there to have a computer completely fake someone's voice or looks. If you search online you will see a video of Taylor Swift selling cookware or Morgan Freeman being Morgan Freeman. These 'deep fake' videos can easily convince you that what you are seeing is real.

As technology advances, deep fake video and audio compilations are going to improve and change the world. Not all the change will be for the good.

People will believe in these videos and follow people to places the real person would have never asked them to go. They will do things in someone else's name and make purchases to feel included in something that a computer animation convinced them of.

This is already a reality. The scenario with Taylor Swift giving away kitchenware has happened; I mean not real Taylor... I think you get it.

You can search for "Morgan Freeman Deep Fake" and you will see a video that looks like a convincing Morgan Freeman. I was impressed.

The current AI engines that make these videos needs to be able to have a lot of source material so stars like Taylor Swift, Morgan Freeman, and Tom Cruise are easy to duplicate. Social media influencers are also prime candidates to be duplicated.

The day is coming soon however, when an AI tool will be able to create videos of any person reading a nursery rhyme in five minutes.

It is a scary new world that we live in.

PLAY ALONG

This chapter's Play Along section will be the easiest one yet.

Task 9-1 Watch a Movie

We would like you to spend a couple hours watching one of the following movies (or all of them if you feel adventurous)...

1. Hackers (1992) [77]
2. The Net (1995) [78]
3. Enemy of the State (1998) [79]
4. Sneakers (2011) [80]
5. Disconnect (2012) [81]
6. Identity Thief (2013) [82]
7. The Beekeeper (2024) [83]

Task 9-2 Review the Movie

Please go on our Facebook or X page and let us know what movie you watched and what you thought of it. If you do not have Facebook or X, please leave us a comment on our website's Contact Us page.

---

[77] Hackers
http://footnote77.dbtwl.com
[78] The Net
http://footnote78.dbtwl.com
[79] Enemy of the State
http://footnote79.dbtwl.com
[80] Sneakers
http://footnote80.dbtwl.com
[81] Disconnect
http://footnote81.dbtwl.com
[82] Identity Thief
http://footnote82.dbtwl.com
[83] The Beekeeper
http://footnote83.dbtwl.com

You can find our social media sites by searching DBTWL on your favorite social media app or by going to www.DBTWL.com and clicking on the application logo.

Facebook[84] and X[85] are the communities we get to most often.

I have given you lots of room to take notes on the movies you watched from this list"

_____

_____

_____

_____

_____

_____

_____

_____

_____

_____

_____

_____

_____

_____

---

[84] Facebook – DBTWL
http://footnote84.dbtwl.com
[85] X – Shayne Kawalilak
http://footnote85.dbtwl.com

CHAPTER 10: SOCIAL MEDIA SECURITY

I have known for a long time that this was going to be one of the most fun chapters to write. It's one chapter that never gets enough coverage in my presentations. In fact, it is one reason I wanted to write this book. I could dedicate an entire full-day workshop to helping people understand how to use social media in a more secure manner.

Doesn't that sound exciting? Well, let's see how you feel about it after you read the chapter.

I want you to realize what I just did at the end of that first paragraph. I included the words 'social media' and 'secure' in the same sentence. Let's be clear, securing social media is a challenge for anyone and the two words should not be used together without significant consideration.

Social Media security does not exist.

Sure, you can make a social media account "more" secure. You can enable MFA on the login. You can make sure all features are in private mode. You can tweak a lot of settings, but you are sharing your life on a free site that makes the bulk of its money by selling information about you to the highest bidder.

This is undoubtedly the one chapter where Charles and I are the farthest apart on the Response Ranking. You have seen by now that Charles and I have many differences in how we reach objectives of personal security.

I have nine children, and in 2008 they started moving out of the house. I immediately went from a place where I knew everything about their lives, to creating a Facebook account to keep up with what they were doing. Still, to this day, someone talks on our family Facebook group 365 days a year.

I am under no illusions that Facebook, X (new and improved Twitter), Instagram, WhatsApp, Tik Tok or other social media platforms, are concerned with protecting my personal information. All these companies make money selling the data that I give them (or allow them to take), or they use it for their own marketing. If they can make a buck selling any information about what I do online, say goodbye to that information.

I know that you've heard this before, but it's worth repeating.

If you are getting a service or product for free, then YOU AND YOUR DATA are the service or product in the transaction.

I am going to try to remember to insert a Time Travel Tip for the most popular Social Media companies because it seems like a popular question online.

TTT – SOCIAL MEDIA POPULARITY

According to Buffer, a social media marketing company, there are 23 social media platforms that they include in their popularity list.[86]

Here is how the apps stack up with the greatest Monthly Active Users (or MAUs)...

- **Face**book (**Meta**) – 3 **Bill**ion
- **What**sApp (**Meta**) – 2.8 **Bill**ion
- **You**Tube (**Alph**abet) – 2.5 **Bill**ion
- **Insta**gram (**Meta**) – 2 **Bill**ion

On the first page of an online search, I found two references to how many children I have and one picture of all nine of them. If we look at Charles's family, we see absolutely nothing. I scrolled through three pages of links and I am drawing a blank.

The problem with people like Charles and my mother not being on social media is sometimes I forget they aren't online. I schedule a poker game or birthday party and put it on social media and assume that everyone I love knows about my event. But that is simply not true. I must make a concerted effort to let people like Charles and my mother know about these events and more, like new grandchildren being born.

You can probably guess that I do not always do this in a timely manner.

Even though Charles and I both agree that simply logging into social media accounts is a threat to your personal privacy, I choose not to let that threat keep me from using social media to communicate with my family or promote my books or speaking engagements. I tell my family and friends how to secure their

---

[86] Social Media Popularity
http://footnote86.dbtwl.com

personal information as much as possible from these companies. Just knowing what they take from your computer can sometimes make people think twice about what they make available online.

If Charles and I both agree that having a social media account is inherently insecure, why do we vary so greatly on our personal experiences with social media?

Five of my children have moved out already and I have six grandchildren living in three countries on two continents. I use the technology that social media offers to remain in contact with this family. I also require social media to promote my various businesses and my writing and speaking career. While I applaud his efforts to avoid social media, it simply isn't something that I am willing to do at this point.

Even with both of us understanding the downside and threats of being on social media, I ended up with several accounts on several platforms (X, Facebook, Instagram, YouTube, Rumble, etc.) and not only does Charles not have an account on one of these platforms, he would never allow me to log into my Facebook account on his computer.

He does not want Meta (Facebook, WhatsApp, Instagram) to know that his computer or his family exist.

EVERYTHING IS FOR SALE

You realize that everything a social media company can get from you is for sale, or you should by now, unless you are reading too fast. I'm not saying it's going to be sold, just that it is up for grabs. Sometimes, if you read the agreements that you check off when you sign up, you will see serious infringements on your privacy that you allowed by simply not unchecking a box.

Put nothing into social media that you wouldn't want your next-door neighbor or a stranger in Quebec to know about.

Do not play games or quizzes on Social Media.

Quizzes and games that your friends share on social media should scare the crap out of you. If your friend shares a quiz with you and it looks interesting and you click on it, a small box pops up and asks you if you want to grant some permissions to the quiz. These permissions are not all required to play, stop and read the check boxes.

There will undoubtedly be one or two that are required at the top, but then there will be several optional boxes. If one of them says "contact and communication history with friends" and it is checked off by default, you should worry. You need to consider that when your friend played this game, they may have left this checkbox on and given away information about you.

Did you hear what I just said?

The social media company may have given away your private information with your friend's permission, not yours. You need to know what is at stake here. You cannot secure your personal information if your friends can give it away without asking or informing you.

STORY TIME – FACEBOOK GAME

I want you to read a blog about a friend that played a fun game that went through her Facebook profile and showed what words she typed the most over the years. She then posted the results on her Facebook profile, where a friend commented about this friend giving away her personal data by playing the game.

This other friend was correct, but not entirely.

This encouraged friend 2 to join the conversation. Friend 2 included screenshots of the game (yes, they played it too) where the game's default permission was to collect the friend's data, but also an obscene amount of data from her friends. That would be friend 2 and her friend that commented. The game was not only collecting the player's information but as much as Facebook would allow it to collect from the player's friends.

It is definitely worth the read. Check the footnote for the link or the **www.DBTWL.com** website.[87]

Some of these games and quizzes are owned in whole or in part by the Chinese Communist Party (or the CCP). I will let you determine which applications fit in this barrel, but you need to understand that there are no laws governing these companies. They do and say whatever the CCP tells them, and you have as little recourse as your government would have in effecting change, basically none.

I have a personal interest in games.

Let's talk about a game I play on my phone with my four youngest sons. I try to get on for 15 minutes every day, but recently they updated their privacy policy and in going through it they asked for permission to give my personal data from my phone to hundreds of advertising companies and big tech companies.

Going through all these companies takes a long time, but while unchecking all their permissions, there are some companies that have a box checked that says, "Legitimate Interest". Because I would love to be a 2 on the Response Rank, I need to know what this is. Here is their word-for-word description…

"How does legitimate interest work? Some vendors are not asking for your consent, but are using your personal data on the basis of their legitimate interest."

---

[87] Facebook Privacy Blog
http://footnote87.dbtwl.com

Let that sink in. Some companies don't need my permission to access my phone or personal information because they have a 'legitimate interest', meaning what? That they really want it. How is this allowed?

In 2021, Facebook announced that it was going to stop allowing third parties (like games and quizzes) to collect certain types of information about Facebook members. I heard so many people commend Facebook for this announcement, but I constantly pointed out that Facebook has not stopped collecting this information, they have just made their customers (those third-party games) start paying Facebook for the information now.

Your data is no more secure than it was last week, but now Facebook has an additional revenue stream. Unless you owned part of Facebook, why were you celebrating?

So, Charles and I agree on the inherent insecurity of social media applications. But while we both know how insecure they are, I limit the specific information that I put on social media, and Charles eliminates it completely.

I totally understand his position and don't discount it in the slightest. It makes sense. But here I am with accounts on Facebook, X, LinkedIn, Instagram, Tik Tok, Rumble, YouTube, etc. Between them, I have fifteen social media accounts for my author profiles, my speaking business, my other ventures, my volunteer work, my professional profiles, and my personal life.

I don't make it easy for these companies to track me, but I make it possible to grab an obscene amount of data from me.

STORY TIME - FACEAPP

FaceApp is a mobile application that many famous people were using back in 2017. As Hollywood celebrities used the app to share photos of themselves artificially aged, people were pointing out that the FaceApp terms of Service included lines like this…

"You grant FaceApp a perpetual, irrevocable, nonexclusive, royalty-free, worldwide, fully-paid, transferable sub-licensable license to use, reproduce, modify, adapt, publish, translate, create derivative works from, distribute, publicly perform and display your User Content and any name, username or likeness provided in connection with your User Content in all media formats and channels now known or later developed, without compensation to you."

Taylor Swift may have thought it was funny to share photos of what she might look like 30 years in the future, but did she do so with any regard to her privacy?

Every selfie that she took could have been uploaded to a server in Russia, and now they have complete access to use them as they choose. Miss Swift would be choked if she found out that some Russian company was printing Taylor Swift calendars and selling them.

How would she feel when she found out that she had no legal right to prevent this company from selling calendars or anything with her photos?

See the above rights that you have in communist China. You have the same rights in communist Russia.

At least one user made a claim that FaceApp was uploading other photos from mobile devices as well. We have no corroboration, but that thought should scare some people.

As an IT professional that has helped many people with their mobile devices, I can tell you that a lot of them have... well... what if Taylor Swift had inappropriate pictures on her phone? I know, nobody ever took pictures on their phone that they wouldn't mind sharing on the internet. Nope. Never.

I cannot implore you enough. You need to read and edit all the permissions of applications you use on your social media platforms and mobile devices. Or just stay away from them. If you are not willing to read these terms of service, you should not be playing with the applications.

You can search for many stories and although this one isn't my favorite, the USA Today article covers a lot of bases.[88]

NOT JUST GAMES

Don't think that only free games or apps try to steal your information either. Google has been clear on more than one occasion that your privacy means little to them. Still today, they scan every word in every email that Gmail users send and receive.

Microsoft scans and views every picture that you save on your OneDrive. They have stated in many places that they don't infringe on your privacy, but they also state that they will cancel your account if you store child pornography on their servers.

While I applaud them for doing anything to prevent the spread of child abuse, the only way they would know what you are storing is to be viewing or scanning it.

Big tech makes a significant amount of money, taking as much data from you as you will allow, knowingly, or otherwise.

You also need to be aware of the data that you give away when you respond to funny posts on social media that tell you to replace your birth month, birth date, and favorite color with funny phrases to get your Norse Viking Name or some other name that would interest you.

When you give these answers, anyone can reverse the info to see your birthday and favorite color. You just gave away info that should be very private.

---

[88] FaceAPP
http://footnote88.dbtwl.com

PLAY ALONG

In the play along section of this chapter, we are going to play with social media. If you are one of those people who don't have a single account on social media, consider yourself way ahead of the curve here. You are already winning, and you can skip to the next chapter.

Task 10-1 Review Privacy Settings

Choose the site that you use most (Facebook is the one I'll use) and go through the privacy settings. It might shock you to see what you are revealing to people who don't even have an account on the platform.

We will post some instructions for some sites on www.DBTWL.com to help you out. Keep in mind that these sites change their links often but we will try to keep up.

Task 10-2 Backup Your Social Media Account.

One thing that I recommend for people like me who can't seem to live without social media accounts is to back them up regularly. I know too many people who said the wrong thing and suddenly their account was closed.

If the President of the United States can have his account shut down on a social media platform, then anything is possible.

If you have a local backup of every post you ever made, and every picture you ever uploaded, you will have much less stress when Meta or Alphabet lock you out of Facebook or YouTube one day.

At least once or twice a year, I sit down and backup my Facebook and X accounts. You should do the same. Instructions change often, but try this to see if it works…

Twitter (X)... on the left menu select More > Settings & Privacy > Your Account > Download an archive of your data

Facebook... click your picture (account) > Settings & Privacy > Meta Accounts Center > under Account settings select Your information and permissions > Download your information.

Once you create a backup, you may have to wait a day to download it, but you will be notified when it is ready.

Task 10-3 Let Us Know How It Went

Join us on our Facebook page (but do NOT create an account for us if you don't have one yet) and let us know how your backup process went. Had you ever backed up your profile before this?

Facebook group: http://footnote84.dbtwl.com

_____

_____

_____

_____

_____

_____

_____

_____

_____

_____

CHAPTER 11: HITTING CLOSER TO HOME

Spam didn't start with the internet. You just don't remember it because we used to call it junk mail. Do you remember the Columbia House 20-CDs-for-a-penny offers? How about Publisher's Clearing House offering you the chance at winning millions of dollars? Half my mail used to be addressed to "Resident" like he was a roommate who never helped with the bills.

We have only talked briefly about protecting data that gets printed to paper and I cannot stress the importance of ensuring that your paperwork at home be shredded. Anything that comes in the mail needs to be handled like it's valuable, even if it just has your name on it.

The proliferation of email happened so fast that many of us were getting spam in our email inboxes as fast as real emails.

Lately, there has been an inordinate amount of spam coming from cell phones. Who hasn't received a text or a phone call warning that a package has arrived, we owe money on duty for a recent purchase, or we have been overcharged for something and we have a refund coming?

I was talking to someone last month while at a client site, and they told me about a text they received for a refund they had to claim, and I told the person that it was a scam.

"But how would they know that I just purchased something from Amazon? Have I been hacked?"

I told the person to reply and ask what purchase they are referring to. It's likely that you haven't been hacked. There has been no compromise. They are simply guessing because virtually everyone in the US and Canada has "just" ordered something from Amazon.

A month ago, I was sitting down in a restaurant with some business partners when I showed them a spam text I just received at the restaurant. It included a tracking link for a parcel I recently ordered.

I laughed and showed them the website link and they all looked at it with suspect eyes since I just told them it was spam. Not one of them noticed the most obvious red flag. Everything on the page looked proper and official, except the large brown and yellow "USP" logo.

How on earth could you spell UPS wrong?

Remember the Red Flag discussion? These are not the bad guys from the movies. These guys are not the master criminals from the best-selling novels.

To make a long story short, I wish my cell phone number wasn't out there, but it is, and I need to use it for too many ventures to slow this spam down.

Before we get into the biggest problem with cell phones, we want to take a moment to talk about saving some money.

CREDIT CARD SAFETY

We need to make a quick comment about having a credit card number stored in your phone. Convenience seems like a requirement today.

I don't think this is a great idea. I have a credit card in my phone, but only one. I get the convenience and if you use it often, add one card to your phone, but not all of them.

I store all my credit card info in the same password manager that we spoke of in **Chapter 3: Password-itis**.

It may be a pain in the butt to type an extra password occasionally, but there are four quick reasons storing credit card info on a phone, laptop, or a browser is a bad idea to me.

1. You will find geeks who disagree with me, but I have seen hackers do amazing things and I honestly believe that anything stored on a local device can be compromised if it is worth enough money. Sometimes, hackers just need a challenge.
2. You do not have access to this information on other devices, which is a significant selling point for some of the password applications. If your phone dies or goes missing, so did your access to your credit card.
3. Your credit card data is now susceptible to being given up by a device, and not necessarily to you. We will talk about that more in this chapter's Story Time.
4. This is one more thing you need to think about if you ever want to change browsers or devices. That credit card info may need to be exported (usually in plain text, making it even more susceptible).

You might not realize how much I dislike using a virtual wallet on my mobile device, but I do trust Android (Google) and Apple to secure my credit cards much more than I would trust a browser or website, no matter who owned them.

Keep in mind that many credit cards now offer "virtual" cards which allow you to 'create' a different number for online shopping to protect your real card number and personal information from online retailers. [89]

I save my credit card info in a password manager and have no issue with this. My credit card info is worth so much less than some of my other credentials.

It would probably not surprise you at all to know that Charles (a strong 2) does not use virtual wallets on his iPhone or his Android. I would be curious to know if there are any self-proclaimed 2's out there who do use them. Let us know on your favorite social media app or by contacting us on the www.DBTWL.com website.

Have you ever heard of Paul Davis? He is a renowned social media and cyber-bullying educator that your kids may have seen at their school. Mr. Davis recently posted on Facebook that he saw someone on a flight this week with no security on their phone. No PIN. No swiping shape. Not even using a fingerprint or facial recognition. Just turn it on and start using the phone.

He claims to see this a lot on flights. I'll be watching for this myself moving forward. If you have children, I recommend that you follow him on social media (once again, only if you already have social media accounts). His information will be at the back of the book as well as on our website.

---

[89] Virtual Credit Cards
http://footnote89.dbtwl.com

Whether you use **Android** or IOS, please secure your **phone** with a **PIN** or a **swipe** shape to lock the screen. It may be annoying to always have to unlock but if you have no lock on your phone, you are automatically either an F (which you should no longer be able to claim if you read this far) or you are a 5. Neither is a safe place to be today and you need to up your game in this one place without hesitation.

If you are interested in having a **Response Ranking** of a 2 or 3, you should be modifying your PIN from the default 4-digits as well. Go ahead and use at least 7 or 8 characters to unlock your phone.

STORY TIME – CREDIT CARD GAMER

I remember hearing a story from a mother at one of my events. A geek at a store in a mall promised her that her credit card would be secure in her phone when they set it up for her. She trusted them, so she entered her credit card information and gave her phone to her child to play a game while they were on vacation.

During the game, there was a way to purchase a free token to the next level, and all you had to do was click on a button… but then this security feature popped up requiring the phone's facial recognition to proceed. Being a smart child, she held the phone in front of her sleeping mother's face. Free game tokens!

If I recall from the story, the child pointed the phone at her mother over 50 times that night and racked up hundreds of dollars on her credit card, and she didn't even notice for a month. It took another few weeks to figure out where the charges came from and what date they were made before she even asked her pre-teen daughter about it.

She did not get the money back because her phone used that wonderful biometric security system. Remember how big a fan I was of this from **Chapter 6: Security 2.0**? Both the credit card company and phone company said the credit card info was secure, and she was responsible for the charges.

ANOTHER PROBLEM WITH CELL PHONES

There is one more thing that you need to be wary of with cell phones we haven't mentioned yet. Did you know that the number of photos goes up by 10% each year? The number of photos in the world doubles every decade. Currently, that puts us around 1.7 trillion photos (yes with a "T") for 2022, bringing the world total up over 12 trillion.

By the end of 2024 we will be taking 1.9 trillion photos per year with over 14 trillion total photos in existence.

Less than 10% of photos end up online, shared in so many ways from email to social media.

Here is the number that shocked me, and the reason I am even talking about pictures in this book. More than 90% of all photos taken this year will be taken with a smartphone. That number is crazy, but why do you care?[90]

Have you ever heard of geotagging?

By default, most smartphones include geospatial information for each photo. This means that when you post a picture, anyone with that image can tell you exactly where it was taken. They used to need to load it into a map program or photo service like Flickr, but now Facebook drops it on a map for everyone too.

You might not have a crazy ex or a secret stalker watching for just such a lucky break, but maybe you are in witness protection or your boss doesn't want the world to know the location of a photo you shared.

I have had issues with clients needing to remove images of work sites from the internet. This is not a simple thing to do. Once a photo

---

[90] Photo Statistics
http://footnote90.dbtwl.com

has been shared online, you can never guarantee that it has been
completely removed, even if you removed it from the first site it was
uploaded to.

STORY TIME – AFGHANISTAN MISTAKE

Imagine that you were a US soldier in Iraq and several brand-new
shiny Apache helicopters show up at your base. You take some
pictures of these sweet new rides and post them to your social media
account like a proud father.

Now imagine, if you will, that an Iraqi who doesn't like you or
your shiny new helicopters sees your picture and loads it into a map
and notices that you left geotagging turned on.

That geotagging feature shows where you took the picture, usually
to within a few meters of accuracy. That information is valuable to
someone who doesn't have access to see into your military base but
would love to know where your new helicopters are parked.

Now, for the story's sake, let's imagine that this Iraqi and his
friends lobbed a barrage of mortar shells at the exact location of your
picture. Imagine how unhappy your bosses would be if they found
out that four helicopters were destroyed because you posted a picture
to social media.

The worst thing about this story is not the permanent record that
would be on that soldier's personnel file. The worst thing about this
story is that it is absolutely true. The US government, hence, the US
taxpayers, lost $124 million worth of helicopters that day, all due to
geotagging on a photo from a smartphone.[91]

---

[91] Story Time – Geotagging
http://footnote91.dbtwl.com

SHARING

I am sure that there are plenty of stories about how geotagging helped a criminal engage a target, from breaking into a home or business, to stalking a pretty girl they found online. There are countless stories of children being kidnapped due to geotagged photos posted online and murders committed with the help of the victim's photos and posts on social media.

Now that you are aware of this threat, hopefully you will do something about it.

My goal is not to make you afraid to take a picture again, but to make you aware of the information that the picture might hold about you and make you think twice about sharing it with that information exposed.

There are benefits to geotagging, but since that is not what this book is about, let me ask you if you even knew that geotagging existed before reading this chapter. If not, then there should be no discussion. You didn't know that this was a feature, so you should not be using it.

If you had heard of it before, and you still weren't using it, then you should have no issue with disabling it on your phone or camera (yes, many new cameras have the feature as well).

OVERSHARING

This chapter is about hitting close to home and pictures are a lot more dangerous than just geotagging allows.

There is no shortage of stories about people who shared photos of a family vacation while they were on vacation and their photos told nefarious people that their home was empty. We don't want to tell you to stop sharing vacation photos, we just want to convince you to wait until you get home to share them.

The police apprehended a group of art thieves in Houston in 2019, who surfed social media for people posting vacation photos instead of driving through neighborhoods looking for dark houses.[92]

As bad as losing hundreds of thousands in art would be, imagine if the thieves arrived to find one of your children stayed home to watch the house. Maybe you don't have that kind of valuable art hanging around. Maybe you need to be worried about repo-men who have been using social media to find vehicles for over a decade now.[93]

Sharing to the world that you are doing something somewhere just takes time away from you doing that thing. Share these great stories when you return home. Nothing good can come from bad people knowing your travel schedule.

ONE LAST WARNING ABOUT MFA

There is one more thing I need to say about cell phones.

They have little screens. They are tiny compared to computers and laptops today.

This is important because of the MFA discussion we had back in Chapter 6: Security 2.0. Do you remember when I said that MFA was not foolproof? Were you wondering how on earth someone could hack it?

If you receive an email from Microsoft to change your password (this should be a red flag on its own), and you open it on your phone, you have a tiny browser window compared to what you see on a computer or laptop. That tiny screen doesn't always give you the clearest view of the webpage URL or the address up top.

---

[92] Social Media Theft Ring
http://footnote92.dbtwl.com
[93] Social Media Repo Men
http://footnote93.dbtwl.com

If the address says **microsoft**online.com or **offic**e.com then you might be just fine, but if the address bar says https://www.microsfot.com/ (with the **F** and **O** reversed) then you have a problem. This is called a man-in-the-middle attack.

Someone sent you a phishing email from **microsfot** and you didn't notice it was spelled wrong (for the record, **Micro**soft owns that domain now).

The issue with cell phones is that these tiny screens make it more difficult to see the full website and see if it is misspelled.

There are three key components to being able to beat this attack...

1. **Educate yourself** as you are doing right now. Move yourself as close as you can to a Knowledge **Ranking of B or A**. This will help you notice red flags.
2. **Always review the URL** of any site, regardless of the difficulty of reading because of the small screen and be on alert for addresses that are similar.
3. **Open a browser** and go to a bookmarked site or click on the site from a search engine rather than clicking on a link in an email or text message.

Keep in mind that Google has been caught allowing hackers to advertise on their search engine numerous times so the 'sponsored' links are not always safe. I do not want to highlight Google because it is a common issue and one that almost caught my family due to an advertisement on **Face**book.

BACK TO PASSWORD MANAGERS

Back at the end of <u>Chapter 3: Password-it</u>is I promised I was going to give you one more reason to use a password manager and I believe that I saved the best for last.

We just spoke about how you could get tricked into filling in your email address and password on www.microsfot.com mistaking it for www.microsoft.com and before you say that it could never happen to you, I will tell you that it happens to the best of us.

It happens when we are in a hurry or not paying attention. That is where a password manager comes in as your last line of defense.

If you were used to a password manager filling in all your credentials and the hackers website is just waiting for you to send your great password, you might not even see a red flag. But if you are waiting for your password manager to autofill your username and password on the SFOT site, you will be waiting all day.

The password manager does not have saved credentials for microsfot, it has saved credentials for Microsoft. The fact that your password manager has no save accounts for the site you just opened, should be a huge red flag for you.

This one feature alone should make it worthwhile setting up an account on a password manager and adding the extension to your web browser.

Was I right when I said that it would be worth the wait?

SHREDDING

Some things that you share are unintentional. In **Chapter 9: Smooth Criminals**, we talked about shredding your papers. We want to take a moment to discuss what papers you need to shred and help you develop a system to eliminate it all.

You need to set a box, bin, or some special place for collecting papers that need to be shredded. When this is full, you shred. It is a simple solution to seriously affect the likelihood of you being a victim of identity theft or another crime.

You also don't even need a shredder. Most offices have one they don't mind you using for personal shredding. Check with your boss or accountant or ask your significant other to do so.

You can also look for a public offering. Most communities have a public event sponsored by a company that will shred everyone's paper for free. In our local community, our auto association (the AMA) hosts free shredding events throughout the year.

As an alternative, a firepit will do the job as well. In our home, we shred all our personal information and then take the bags to the lake and use the shredded paper as fire starter.

To prove to you, that a 2 and a 4 are not just a separation for professional geeks, but that our Response Ranking is more of a state of mind, I will confess that Charles (a 2) and I (a 4) shred the same paper.

Charles basically shreds anything with his name on it. I used to only shred items with more than my name on it. I always figured if someone was going through my trash that they already knew my name and address. I focused on preventing papers from leaving my home or office that had my birthday, an account number, or other identifiable data.

After a discussion about this chapter with Charles, I concluded that all identifiable information should be shredded. If my paper blows out of a recycling truck or the municipal dump, my name and address on an envelope now provide identifiable information to someone who knew neither part a minute earlier.

You are not the only person who might learn something new from this book. But I am a 4, sometimes I need to hear things more than once to take heed.

It turns out that my wife is much closer to Charles's 2 than I suspected on this matter. When we were discussing this, she mentioned she wasn't as disciplined as she should be and that sometimes she misses shredding a magazine cover.

It had never occurred to me to shred a magazine cover.

I called Charles to ask where he draws the line. I found it hilarious that in his list of items that he shreds, he included several items I never considered, including magazine covers. He shreds anything with his name, address, or any other identifiable data, including the envelopes they came in as they might have a barcode with data.

On a bright note, Charles and my wife have saved me a couple of hours a year sifting through my sorting pile, an activity I do every couple of months to ensure that I am shredding enough paper. Now I will just shred the whole pile without further review. How liberating.

This bin includes any paper with the following information:

- The name of anyone in my family
- Any address or account information
- Any personal information at all

These items will include:

- Magazine covers
- Envelopes,
- Bills,
- Junk mail,
- Receipts (unless the item is still under warranty),
- Pay stubs,
- Christmas cards that don't get saved.

TTT — SHREDDING BEST PRACTICES

We will post a great link to the www.DBTWL.com website under The Book > Chapter 11 > Time Travel Tips and if we ever see a better site or list, we will update this information so you are always kept up to date with the most current or relevant information.

If you aren't sure of what to shred, you can find some extensive lists online. Currently I am promoting the TimeShred.com list.[94]

Be sure to sign up on our website to join our mailing list so you are informed when we do updates.

VIDEO

Now that we have covered the danger of photos, let's chat briefly about videos from webcams. I promised we would continue this in Chapter 8: A Fresh Can of Spam, when I told you about Cassidy Wolf, Miss Teen USA 2013.

If you remember her story, you remember that someone hacked her device, and the criminal could live stream video from it.

Many webcams today have covers built into the device to prevent such a thing. I am sure some smartphones have a physical cover as well. If your device doesn't have a physical cover allowing you to manually cover the camera lens, please make one right now with a post-it note, tape, or tissue draped over the camera.

These camera covers are available online at many outlets.

WHAT IS A VPN?

Before we wrap up this chapter, I need to talk briefly about a subject that has come up in many Q&A sessions at my presentations.

---

[94] Shred List
http://footnote94.dbtwl.com

You may hear people say that you should use a VPN on your computer or mobile device to do your browsing. VPN stands for Virtual Private Network. A VPN encrypts your complete browsing session from one end to another. I rarely use VPNs, and Charles only opts for them when he must use public Wi-Fi in hotels and similar situations.

When Charles uses a VPN, he uses one that he manages that connects his laptop to his home so that all his browsing is encrypted in a tunnel under his complete control.

We both have concerns about using a VPN from an online service. The VPN connection is encrypted from point A to point B. One of those points is on your computer. The problem is that you often have no idea where the other point is. There is nothing to stop the VPN provider from ending the VPN at their office and calling that Point B, then forwarding the traffic to your destination.

This allows them to record what you do and hand it to anyone they want, including government agencies who should not be spying on you.

The "P" in VPN stands for "private" and if history is any guide, it may be anything but private. The number of companies that have given VPN information to government agencies is stunning.[95]

If you use a VPN service, you will get a false sense of security. Your traffic may be encrypted, but not past the endpoints. If you do not own the VPN, that false sense of security could end up causing you to do things that put your personal data at risk.

---

[95] VPN companies
http://footnote95.dbtwl.com

PLAY ALONG

Task 11-1 Geotagging

The first thing we are going to do in this play-along section is remove geotagging on your smartphone. You can always reactivate it later if you find a need to have it, but for now, let's disable it to protect this one small part of your personal privacy.

You can go to the www.DontBeTheWeakestLink.com website or www.DBTWL.com and click on The Book > Chapter 11 > Play Along for instructions on how to disable geotagging on both Android and Apple devices.

You can also test your new search skills and open a web browser and search for "disable geotagging" plus the model of your cell phone. You should get a couple of great and simple tutorials.

Task 11-2 Shredding

If you do not have a shredder at home, go online to find a free shredding service for personal files. There should be someone in your area offering this as a free service.

Start saving papers that need to be shredded. Create a space for a pile, box, bin, etc. so that you can start forming good habits today with your personal printed information.

_____

_____

_____

_____

CHAPTER 12: BONUS - CAMBRIDGE ANALYTICA

It's time to get scandalous. I wanted to add a commentary on the Cambridge Analytica scandal, and I am disgusted at how much time I wasted trying to fit it into a previous chapter. Then I realized, this is not an issue with social media so much as it is an issue with education. It needs its own chapter!

Since education is one of the key purposes of the book, let's jump into it and ignore my wasted time. We can call it an investment if it makes you feel better. I tried. It didn't help me at all.

We are going to do an analysis of the data you give to big tech and hopefully you have already learned enough to make more secure choices. This isn't a simple thing to teach because social media companies change privacy settings more often than politicians change their minds.

You know you can never protect the data that you put in that account 100%, and everything that they talk about in relation to security and privacy is questionable. On top of that, few governments are holding them accountable.

I don't know if you have seen the documentary called *The Great Hack,* but the Cambridge Analytica scandal should make you aware of two things…

1. You willingly and unknowingly hand over more data than you ever imagined.
2. Your data is being used in ways that you never intended,

Charles and I agree The Great Hack was more of a witch hunt than a documentary, but we didn't agree wholly on the hidden agenda of the production. Here is a company that paid an obscene amount of money for data sets from big tech companies (mostly Facebook). Cambridge Analytica had a database of hundreds of millions of people. Easily billions of points of data, from your favorite color to your usual time on social media, and even what time you went to bed. They had information from your cell phones, tablets, and laptops and they knew your browsing histories and what videos you watched.

All the information from <u>Chapter 1: Find Your Weakness</u> is for sale, plus a lot more. This data is for sale from companies like Meta (through Facebook, Instagram, WhatsApp) and Alphabet (Google, Chrome, Android) but we can't forget about Apple (iPhone, iWatch, iTunes), Microsoft (Windows, Edge, Xbox), Amazon (Prime Video, Twitch, Audible, IMDb, etc.). This list could be another book.

And one more time for the people in the back row…

If you are getting a service or product for free, then YOU AND YOUR DATA are the service or product in the transaction.

One issue with social media is that it allows third-party apps to take data on their own. On this account, companies like Cambridge

Analytica didn't need to take data directly from Facebook because they convinced hundreds of thousands of people to play a game or do a quiz.

I understand if you watched that video to learn more about the evil empire of Facebook and Mark Zuckerberg. If you watched it without an open mind, you might not have seen the evil empire that poisoned an innocent woman to turn her to the dark side.

The show is primarily about three people, a journalist named Carole Cadwalladr, a Cambridge Analytica employee named Brittany Kaiser, and David Carroll, a private citizen who sued Cambridge Analytica for not providing him with the data they had on him.

Cambridge Analytica is a company, or was a company, that made its money by using the data that it compiled to influence political discussions. I do not agree with the ethics of their business model, but I also am unclear as to what law people think they broke in the USA?

As much as I hate the misuse of personal information, my opinion is that they didn't do as much wrong as the producers of *The Great Hack*. One scene in the documentary shows a clip from the *Late Night with Seth Meyers* talkshow, where the host says, "Really Facebook? You forgot to mention that 50 million people had their private data breached, but every time it's my uncle's friend's sister's dog's birthday, I get a notification."

I have two noteworthy issues with this statement. First, it implies that Facebook was hacked, and their users didn't voluntarily give out this information, which is a huge stretch of reality. Second, virtually every one of these people involved with *The Great Hack* had no issue when the same data was used to help Barack Obama get elected.

> If you only believe that an action should be criticized when it benefits people you don't like, then your perception of the action divides the people, not the action itself.

At one point you hear from a young pink-haired gentleman named Christopher Wylie (another ex-employee of Cambridge Analytica). He confesses that he believes that what Cambridge Analytica did was "a grossly unethical experiment". That's a quote.

He believed it was acceptable to help a Democrat win an election but utterly disgusting to help a Republican?

That does not make Christopher Wylie a whistleblower, it makes him a hypocrite.

You may have noticed that Barack Obama used these big tech data points to defeat Bernie Sanders in the Democrat primaries and then to help put Barack Obama into the Whitehouse. As a matter of fact, Brittany Kaiser had a huge personal role in this.

You might remember one line when Brittany Kaiser is listening to audio recordings of meetings, and she says it was like "a criminal admitting to everything he's done wrong around the world".

Viewers seem to be missing the obvious point that these people are just 21st century "ad men". For longer than any of us have been alive, advertising companies have been bending truth, lying, and abusing any information they could acquire in the name of selling something.

Brittany said at one point that "data surpassed oil in its value", but that statement isn't as true in the sense that the documentary made it sound. Data may be worth more now, but it is not because data hasn't had more individual value than petroleum in the past. Ask a spy if data was valuable 100 years ago. The dramatic change is that the quantity of oil is barely rising every year, but the quantity of data is exploding exponentially, as is the technology that assists in our capture and use of it.

My thoughts? **Cambridge Analytica** had no morals or ethics in how it collected and used peoples' data. It was simply a business.

Some might believe that **Carole Cadwalladr** doesn't use morals or ethics to guide her writing, and she does seem to bend everything to her political bias.

Brittany Kaiser has a clear bias in everything that she seems to say and do. She too could be questioned as to whether she uses morals or ethics in much of her life at all, as she accepts actions and beliefs from her surroundings so long as they benefit her or the people that she deems worthy.

David Caroll may not be as morally corrupt as others invested in this documentary, but he clearly states that the data abuse did not bother him until after he realized it helped get **Donald Trump** elected, which matches the hypocrisy of others in the documentary. Regardless of whether you liked Trump before or after or ever, using people's personal information to affect election results is either wrong, or it isn't.

I suspect that **David Caroll** is more hypocrite than hero.

Using this data is either acceptable to you or it isn't. It can't be only acceptable if it helps the team you like or you are the hypocrite, not the guys using the data.

As authors of this book, we do not wish to influence your political leanings. As a matter of disclosure, **Charles** and I have voted for radically different and opposing candidates on occasion. Our aim is simply to educate you on what data you are exposing, and what the outcomes of that exposure might be. If you feel so inclined, the information in this book should aid you in sharing less of your personal data in the future.

Do not consider whether you would approve of this information being used in specific ways. Determine whether you think it is okay for it to be used at all. Whether laws will continue to make it harder for companies to collect your data or not, will not prevent these companies from collecting it.

> The first and most important step to securing your personal data is for you to educate yourself and
> understand what they are taking and how they are taking it.

ADVERTISING

We spoke extensively about ad revenue in **Chapter 4: Join the Search** but I believe it deserves some repetition.

If you aren't convinced that advertising is significant for a company like Amazon, consider that they generate more revenue from advertising than any other department. AWS (**Amazon Web Services**) surpassed retail in sales and profit a few years ago. In 2021, AWS brought in $62B in sales with an operating income of $18.5B. Because of the high cost of hardware and skilled labor to keep the AWS cloud system running, their profit is much less than their revenue.

Amazon collected over $31B in advertising revenue for the same period and although they didn't release the expenses of that department, I imagine it is a fraction of the AWS group, likely making advertising the most profitable group in the company. [96]

Amazon takes home 14.4% of US digital ads making it the third largest online advertiser behind Google (25.2%) and Meta (20.4%). If your personal information is the key to personalized advertising, then your personal information is worth a lot of money to these companies and many others, like **Cambridge Analytica**. [97]

---

[96] Amazon Ad Profit
http://footnote96.dbtwl.com
[97] Amazon advertising market share
http://footnote97.dbtwl.com

Whether you have social media accounts, need to shop online, or spend hours a day on the internet, you now have the knowledge at your disposal to modify how you respond to your new knowledge. Watch for red flags, be more protective of your personal information, and enjoy your time online doing the things that you want to do with the Response Rank that you feel appropriate.

Task 12-1 Watch The Great Hack

Watch the Cambridge Analytica documentary called *The Great Hack*.[98] At the time of editing this book, it was still streaming on Netflix in several countries.

Watch it with an open mind and ask yourself, was it worse that Cambridge Analytica used so much of our personal information for financial gain, that they used that information to influence elections, or that they used it to help someone we didn't vote for to win an election?

Or was the worst thing, that we enable it so easily by giving away such an abundance of our personal information in this digital world... maybe not if you are a 1 or 2 like Charles, but the rest of us.

_____

_____

_____

_____

_____

_____

_____

_____

_____

[98] The Great Hack
http://footnote98.dbtwl.com

ADDITIONAL READING LIST

Online Safety for Grade 3 / 4 / 5 / 6[99]

By Paul Davis

Paul Davis (https://SocialNetworkingSafety.net/)

Paul Davis is a Social Media and Cyber-Bullying Educator who educates children and empowers parents on the topic of Social Networking and Online Safety.

He published his first book in a magazine format in 2020 focusing on lessons for grades 3 through 6. He also does presentations for grades 7 and 8 as well as 9 through 12.

Shayne's take:

Paul Davis doesn't just give presentations to students that change their lives, but he involves parents by doing evening presentations so families can increase their knowledge at the same time as their youth and from the same source. I have seen him travel across Canada but missed him on his last trip to Alberta in November of 2024.

I am very much looking forward to meeting this young man who gives so much to our youth. He also does presentations to businesses and seniors. He has presented to over a million people since 2011.

While I haven't read his magazine yet, I would highly recommend that you follow Paul Davis if you already have a Facebook or X (new Twitter) account, regardless of your parental status…

Facebook: http://pauldavis-fb.dbtwl.com

X: http://pauldavis-x.dbtwl.com

---

[99] Paul Davis magazine
http://footnote99.dbtwl.com

How to Disappear: Erase Your Digital Footprint, Leave False Trails, and Vanish without a Trace [100]

By Frank M Ahearn & Eileen C Horan

Frank M. Ahearn (www.Disappear.info)

Sometime in the mid-eighties while working for an investigative agency, I discovered I had a unique ability to pretext and social engineer; which is lying to extract private information. Eventually, I left my job and opened a skip tracing (finding people) service in some anonymous office in mid-town Manhattan. I spent my days pulling phone records, bank records, travel records, and any other document or file a client needed. My philosophy was, if you can afford it, I can obtain it.

Shayne's take:

I thoroughly enjoyed reading this book. I suppose a part of me wanted to know if I could ever be a 2, like Charles. My Response Ranking could move to a 3 when the kids are all moved out, but I am not sure that I could ever do the whole 2 thing. And I certainly have no interest in ever being a 1, not even if I was old and alone.

Handling short bursts of loneliness are cool with me, and even longer stints if I am busy, but no matter how crappy I think people are, I like to be around them. Frank and Eileen really brought me closer to understanding what could be going through the mind of a 1 or 2 though.

I don't know if their book helps so much with a lot of the topics in our book, but if I wanted to hide from a crazy ex or start a new life for any reason, this is the first thing I would read.

If you have a Spotify Premium subscription, you can listen to this audiobook for free.

---

[100] Amazon bookstore – How to Disappear
http://footnote100.dbtwl.com

The Secret to Cybersecurity: A Simple Plan to Protect Your Family and Business from Cybercrime[101]

By Scott Augenbaum (www.CyberSecureMindset.com)

I am dedicated to helping individuals and businesses succeed by providing them with the knowledge and tools they need to protect themselves from Cybercrime. With my decades of experience as a retired FBI Supervisory Special Agent and my expertise in Cybercrime prevention, I have a unique understanding of the ever-evolving threat landscape.

Shayne's take:

Scott goes into many areas in The Secret to Cybersecurity that we don't touch in DBTWL. It may be the perfect follow-up book, especially if you liked what you read in this one already.

If you think you would enjoy a more professional writing style without getting too anal, then Scott Augenbaum is certainly the man for you. At the very least, I would recommend that you follow Scott on your favorite social media platforms (again, only if you already have an account there). His website above has links to his profiles on Facebook, X, LinkedIn, YouTube, and Instagram.

I would have loved more time to discuss some of what he said in his Social Media and Mobile Device chapters but I was too late for the editor. Scott also covers topics on Real Estate and online dating that you might really enjoy.

My favorite thing about Mr. Augenbaum is his videos on LinkedIn. He doesn't speak down to you or use techie-talk and that is what my wife and mother need. Hopefully you feel the same way.

---

[101] Amazon bookstore – The Secret to Cybersecurity
http://footnote101.dbtwl.com

The Art of Invisibility: The World's Most Famous Hacker Teaches You How to Be Safe in the Age of Big Brother and Big Data[102]

By Kevin Mitnick (www.MitnickSecurity.com)

The world's most famous hacker was also the author of four published books, including the cybersecurity industry primer, The Art of Deception, and the New York Times Bestselling Ghost in the Wires.

From his firsthand experience eluding authorities to his personal take on the biggest threats to our modern digital privacy, readers go inside the one-of-a-kind mind of Kevin Mitnick for a perspective like none other. With the pace of true-crime thrillers, Kevin's books are fun, exciting, and have readable language so everyone can understand.

Shayne's take:

I really enjoyed the book, The Art of Invisibility, and I am currently listening to the audiobook and loving the narration. If you enjoyed reading our book and want to move deeper into what is possible in cybersecurity, this may be a great next book. I would recommend it highly if you have a Knowledge Ranking of a C. Anyone could enjoy it but it goes much deeper into the technology than was our goal with this book.

I tried to find a couple books for you to continue your journey and supply options from an ex-FBI agent and a world-class hacker that was busted by the FBI should definitely provide alternatives for you. To me, the chapter called "The FBI Always Gets Its Man" was worth the purchase price alone.

If you have a Spotify Premium subscription, you can listen to this audiobook for free.

Take some notes about these awesome books…

---

[102] Amazon bookstore – The Art of Invisibility
http://footnote102.dbtwl.com

SPECIAL ACKNOWLEDGEMENTS

This is a section where we give special thanks to the people and companies that assisted so greatly in the creation of this book while keeping ourselves engaged with the Weakest Link Scale.

Their parts were large and larger. There were no small contributions from these people or companies. Hopefully, I expressed how much their contributions have meant to me in the pages that follow.

GER HENNESSY

Ger Hennessy is more of a corrector of othe'rs rightings than a riter in his own wright. He has an I for detail and takes pride in his f forts. He nose somethings about the internet, but tends to keep them to himself. He prefers camping to city breaks, but loves an auld city brake. He is a net contributor to crowd funding, but has not as of yet, contributed a net, or any meshes to speak off.

Shayne's take: Firstly, I need to mention how odd that bio that Ger wrote is going to sound on the audiobook version of Don't Be the Weakest Link. For those people enjoying the audiobook, I will include this bio on our website so you can understand my challenge reading it for yourself.

Ger and I worked together for 10 days on a magazine in Finland. That's it. It was for a Scout Jamboree and we never knew one another before, and have never met again up to the publishing of this book. I am from Canada and he is from Ireland. It would be a rough road trip to go visit him. I was one of four English writers that the magazine brought in and he was my editor.

I instantly clicked with this guy and his command of English was amazing though you would never know from his bio above. He has the Chicago Manual of Style memorized, or possibly tattooed all over his body. I feel like I abused him a little, like my own breathing version of ChatGPT before ChatGPT existed. I was guilty more than once of describing him as "the Irishman who could teach English at Oxford if he so chose".

Ger is pronounced like Germany, but there is only one, like you drop the 'many'. I know, dad's lose their sense of huumor as they age. This Jamboree was way back in 2016 and eight years ago, publishing anything was so far from my mind that it might as well have not existed.

I messaged Ger, who has a technical background in addition to being well-spoken, and asked if he would be interested in editing a book. He was open to the idea and that was November 9, 2019.

I was slightly scared because as much as I loved working with this man, we agree on almost nothing. I honestly cannot think of a single topic that we agree on regarding politics, economics, religion, foreign affairs, etc. You name it, we do not see eye to eye.

I think the reason that we move past it so easily is that one of us is a touch conservative and one of us is a tad liberal. There are no fascists or anarchists in this relationship, just two guys with differing opinions who respect one another for speaking about them. We do not hold back. Often, something big happens and the chat gets a link, "What do you think of this?".

There was slight hesitation in 2020, when I was thinking that the book could really happen. Ger went through the Introduction and Chapter 1 (which has vastly changed since then) but he made one huge correction, which was not really a correction, just a comment. And I said to my wife, "this dude gets me!"

From Chapter 1… my quote was, "Clearly, Charles would not be pleased about his name being exposed on the internet. I, on the other hand, wouldn't care if my name were on a billboard in Times Square."

Ger simply added "so long as it was spelled correctly."

That one line made my soul smile. This man gets me. He really does.

The rest is history.

CHARLES

It's a challenge to write about a person without saying anything.

Charles still doesn't understand why I put his name on the front of this book. He literally has not written a single word between the covers.

While I understand this, I need to somehow convince the reader that any accolades to his contribution to this final product are insufficient. He could have written half the words, and his influence still would not surpass what he did for me just being a sound board. We are talking about hundreds of hours listening to me talk. That could not have been easy.

Then there are the comments that he made that got me thinking differently or deeper about so many things. He started the gears turning and had impact on changing the title of the book and the creation of the Weakest Link Scale.

I can't count the number of times that Charles made a statement that rocked me. I honestly started this book knowing that we were going to agree on everything except how amazing Cisco was as a company and network gear.

Oddly, after five years of work on this book, it seems that our view on Cisco is closer than many other things where I assumed we would be in perfect unison. Sorry Cisco. Clearly that man was corruptible.

MY WIFE

Stacey has probably invested just as much time in listening to me read and write and it had to be so much more boring for her. Charles and I have both been professional geeks for over a quarter century. Stacey is much less familiar with technology. It's not a stretch to say that she hates the stuff.

Considering her disdain for all things tech, she has eagerly jumped on board to assist in any way she could, no matter how technical the requirement.

I will give that woman commendations where deserved and I have never met anyone who could find something online better than she, if there is money involved. I can't think of a single thing in our life that I found a deal on. The house, the lake lot, the boat, the golf cart, every vehicle we have ever owned, every vacation we have ever taken, every hotel we have ever stayed in, the list could go on.

The Google-Fu is strong with this one, I mean the Duck Duck Fu.

At the end of the day, I don't think that my wife has read any other book I wrote, and with all the technology in this one, I am not sure she will ever read this through. She must feel like she has heard the audiobook 5 times already.

As much as I let her do her own thing, I am going to push her to read or listen to this book one more time once it is done. I am sure that she will find it valuable and worthwhile. During the writing of this book, she has moved from an F or a D on the Knowledge Scale to a solid C and I need to know that she is a C+ or even a B before I will be comfortable dying before her.

I wrote the book with her and my mother in mind, so it would be nice to see her learn its lessons.

STEVE WALKER (WALK-THROUGH TECH INC.)

Steve is the big wig behind a medium sized MSP in Edmonton, Alberta.

An MSP is a Managed Service Provider. For companies that are not big enough , or make a choice to not have an internal IT department, an MSP provides technical resources to keep that business running.

MSP's are also great resources to amend a company's in-house IT department for large projects. We go in and help fill resource gaps for expansions, relocations, upgrades, and so forth. IT departments often don't have the bandwidth to add projects which require hundreds of hours to complete if they are already busy.

Since 2016, I have been working with Walk-Through Tech on a part-time and casual basis. My priority is working on the projects that pay for my lifestyle, basically feeding my kids, keeping my boat floating, and keeping my wife happy enough to not want to kill me in my sleep. In between these projects, I offer my time and services to Steve and his clients.

I might not have stayed with Steve so long except that he runs his business with a significant Christian tilt. Early on, he asked my opinion on a solution for a client and wanted to know what was best for their needs. Clearly, the lower cost option solved their needs, but the expensive route would give them additional options and put a lot more money in Steve's pocket.

"But what is best for the client?"

Steve was legitimately asking about the interest of the client, and I had to answer honestly. I didn't know Steve that well and I didn't think I owed him anything, so honesty was my default, "they don't need the additional options, the cost savings would be the better way to go in my mind".

I don't know if that was a test or if he honestly wanted my input, but either way, his authentic concern for the best interests of his client really moved me. This was the beginning of a long business relationship that is still moving forward.

Steve is more than just a pervasive professional geek, he is a Christian, a husband, and a father. And those are some of my favorite things. He is younger than me, so he hasn't had the opportunity to be a grandfather yet, but his time will come.

I always try to be available if Steve needs me for a larger project, but I have taken so much time off the past 2 years to work on this book and for speaking engagements that I cannot fail to mention how much his flexibility has enabled me to follow these ambitions.

With that in mind, on the off chance that someone in the capital region of Alberta reads this book and needs technical support services, Walk-Through Tech might be the perfect fit for you.

Check out Steve and the gang at www.wtti.ca to see if they can help.

INTERNET ARCHIVE

I don't know how many of you have ever heard of Internet Archive or their Wayback Machine, but since 1996, Internet Archive has been archiving webpages, books, audio recordings, etc.

I decided early on that if I was going to write a book about technology that I needed two things. I needed to have a way to continually update people with new information, so I wasn't writing new editions of this book every six months for the rest of my life.

This was answered with the creation of the TTT – Time Travel Tips.

The second thing I needed was to find a way to ensure that the hyperlinks in the footnotes would always work. I will be hosting the footnote links on the www.DBTWL.com website and all the footnote links will point to one of our internal websites so that I can change the redirection if a website was changed or removed from the internet.

If the book has a link to the best search engines in 2025 and then at the end of 2025, we want to update that link, we can just point our site to a new webpage so that our link is always sending you somewhere current.

In the first year of writing this book, three of my main footnotes went to dead links, and one went to an updated Forbes article that had changed the numbers they mentioned. Their update of the article made me look like I couldn't read at all.

This is where Internet Archive's Wayback Machine came in. Rather than point the footnote to our website and redirect it to a website like Forbes that could change or remove their webpage without notice, we would point to Internet Archive's website and the snapshot that they took of that webpage the day that we referenced it.

There are over 100 footnotes in this book and over a dozen of them had to be archived by us for the first time. That means, that Internet Archive, a non-profit that has saved over 900 billion webpages, did not know that these websites in our footnotes were on the internet until we told them. Thus, we added the websites that we needed to make available to you, to their saved archive so that even if Forbes or the New York Times went out of business, shut down their site, or just deleted an article, you would still have the information they published in the past.

One of these footnotes was initially archived on December 9, 2024. Internet Archive didn't know it existed until the week this book was published, and they only knew about it now because I asked them to archive it for this book. Don't Be the Weakest Link should be released before Christmas 2024 and here we are, archiving webpages for footnotes so that you always have the information at your disposal.

The archive created and maintained by this non-profit, allowing user contributions, is essential to this book's status as a prominent reference tool. Unlike sites like Wikipedia, not only can I not change or remove a site in the archive, the original publisher of the site (Forbes or the New York Times maybe) cannot modify or remove anything of theirs that was archived.

Once a site is archived by the Wayback Machine, it is there forever for everyone to view.

I have discussed with the team running the publishing, that a minimum of 1% of profit from the book sales will be donated to Internet Archive so long as the book is in print and using their site. If you have some extra money and are looking for a group worthy of a donation, please consider Internet Archive.

Read more about them here… https://archive.org/about/

BIONIC-READING®

We knew early on that we were going to need a large-print edition of this book. Shayne insisted on it once he started presenting to organizations supporting the elderly. We wanted to ensure that the knowledge contained in these pages was available to everyone and since the elderly are such prevalent targets of hackers, we opted to support them with large print formatting as well.

Shayne has also discussed with us that he wants to support individuals with reading difficulties. He is a huge proponent of Bionic Reading®[103], which basically emboldens the first part of a word to make it easier for brains that struggle with the simple task of reading. This option may help some readers power through and read at higher speeds. It may hinder some readers however, so read a sample on their website before deciding which version you would like.

Shayne's take: I have been blessed and infuriated with ADHD and although the Canadian government classifies it as a mental illness, I have found it to be a huge benefit in my life. While I do struggle with focusing on some tasks that a normal person would hammer out in a fraction of the time, I also have the capability to put my head down and work on a singular task for 18 hours straight… just bring me food and water and watch me go.

The problem is that I must be very interested in the topic and enjoy the work to give it that super-focus.

One thing that I have never been able to focus on like I know I should, is reading. My mind wanders between words and sentences and just forget about what happens when I turn the page.

---

[103] Bionic-Reading®
http://footnote103.dbtwl.com

I used to read in bed with my wife. We would take turns holding a book and read it together. The problem was that she reads twice as fast as I do. Reading together didn't last as long as I would have liked.

If I could go back in time and change one thing in my life, it would not be preventing my divorce (though that really sucked); it would not be preventing the accident that put me in a wheelchair, walker, and a cane for 14 years; and it would not be filing for bankruptcy after losing everything in an accident that financially ruined me for 15 years (thought I still think bankruptcy would have made some things easier).

If I could go back in time and do one thing to improve my life, it would be to go back and learn how to read faster. I do not believe there is a single thing in your life that can have a more significant effect on your future than your love and ability to read.

The brain does some weird things. Have you ever seen this before?

What i if told you,
You the read first line wrong,
Same the with second,
And also the third!

When I see my brain playing tricks on me like this, I assume that somewhere is a hidden secret that will release the ability for me to read faster and improve my comprehension.

"Aoiccrdng to rserecah at Caimbrdge Unvriestiy, it dsoen't mtater in waht oerdr the leettrs in a wrod are, the only ioamprtnt thnig is taht the frist and last letetr be at the right plcae. The rest can be a toatl mses and you can sitll read it wthiout prbloem. Tihs is becasue the hmuan mind does not read eevry lteetr by iteslf but the wrod as a wohle."

The fact that many people can read that paragraph is a testament to the amazing abilities of the human brain. You should read more about the amazing work that Graham Rawlinson did at Cambridge University on this topic. [104]

From www.Bionic-Reading.com: "**Bionic Reading®** is **a new** method **facili**tating **the read**ing **proc**ess **by guid**ing **the eyes through** text **with artif**icial **fixa**tion **points. As a res**ult, **the rea**der **is only** focu**sing on the highligh**ted **init**ial **lett**ers **and lets the brain cent**er **complete the word. In a digit**al **world domin**ated **by shall**ow **forms of read**ing, **Bionic Read**ing® **aims** to **encour**age **a more in-dep**th **read**ing **and underst**anding **of writt**en **cont**ent."

---

[104] Typoglycaemia – Cambridge University
http://footnote104.dbtwl.com

CROWDFUNDING CAMPAIGN

On behalf of Kawali Publishing, I wish to express that nobody will understand how much I appreciate the supporters to our Crowdfunding campaigns.

What is a crowdfunding campaign? We do a pre-sales run for about a month where we sell books on a website called Kickstarter. You can go to www.Kickstarter.com and check out our previous campaigns for a poetry book and a children's book if you search for Kawali Publishing.

http://kickstarter.dbtwl.com

Every campaign has someone who has really stood out for one reason or another and this campaign is no different. Poetry and Children's books have a certain appeal to the general public but people don't go out of their way to look for non-fiction books about internet safety and data privacy very often. I knew this from the beginning, so we worked harder spreading the word of this book on social media and through our email list as well as at in-person events.

The result was that almost every single person who purchased one of these books was known to us… except Julie. Not only is Julie a mystery, but she is also a very generous tipper. When you purchase one of the support levels you can choose an e-book, paperback, hardcover, audiobook, or combination of these. After your selection, you can choose to add a tip which just goes to help the developer of the Kickstarter campaign, in this case, the publisher.

I have to imagine that if you are waiting on Julie at a restaurant tonight, you will be receiving a nice tip if you smile. She was one of 4 people who supported the campaign and also gave a 'bonus' tip with their purchase.

Another real surprise was that we said we were going to print the campaign supporters' names in the back of the book to say thanks. In the campaign survey, we asked how they would like their name to appear. Some chose first initial, some last initial, and some full name. As a shocker though, several said no name or initials.

I don't know if these people are shy or introverted or if they are possibly already a B on the Knowledge Ranking or have a 1 or 2 for a Response Rank. But their names will not be shown on the next page.

The other odd thing that I noticed with the third book is that there were no super-backers. With the other two books we had someone who had backed almost 500 projects, almost 1200 projects, and over 1400 projects. I don't know where these people find the time and money for this, but I appreciate that they do.

CAMPAIGN SUPPORTERS

In the order of their support for our campaign:

- Anonymous
- Ashley Carlyle
- Anonymous
- Julie K
- S MacKay
- C McDonald
- P Schiffner
- My son Ryan
- Noel K
- Anonymous
- Queen Karla
- Billy Rose Falcon

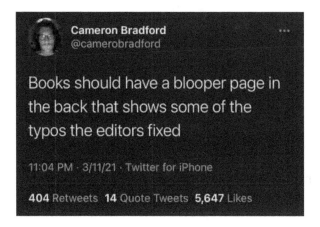

THE BLOOPER REEL

One thing I really miss about DVDs was the commentary videos and the blooper reels. I guess that's two things. When I saw the post above on Twitter a few years ago I fell in love with the idea, and it just simmered.

When Ger was done with the edits, and I was going through them I knew that some of them were being saved for the back of this book. In case you thought the topic of the book was too heavy, I want to ensure that you close this book with a smile.

The dedication page was blank for a long time and this was the placeholder…

This book is dedicated to someone for something.

GER: (like its author who faffed around on it for over 4 years)

Shayne gives his money to more people online

GER: "many people".

If "more" means "more than Shayne", then it's redundant, and confusing.

GER: if I use a password manager, why make my passwords memorable instead of something like *ISHI&DjkDN<DIUkenfO8s|9

SHAYNE: *ISHI&DjkDN<DIUkenfO8s|9 is easier for a computer to guess than "Ger is a great Editor but 2 times a week I would like to remember this password!"

There were definitely points in the book where it was great to have another geek as an editor…

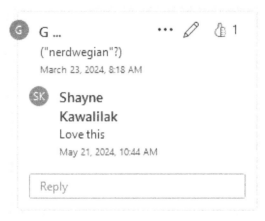

GER: counter-point, you're on the bus to the cinema, but need to book tickets, is it more likely that your info will be stolen because you're reading your Card number and cvv, and typing it out in a public place, and then putting the card back into your wallet, or that your phone will be hacked and your payment details stolen...

SHAYNE: Added a line at the bottom

GER: "Tom Hiddleston used biometrics in The Avengers"

SHAYNE: But I want more retro movies

GER: So it's not just that they want your valuable data or precious family memories, they're happy to prevent you from accessing your own data, safe in the knowledge that you'll consider paying to get your precious family memories back.

SHAYNE: Adjusted with a couple lines about London Drugs

A ransomware attack hit St. Margaret's Health in 2021. SMP Health, the parent organization of St. reported that they were

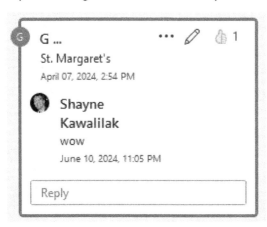

BOOK: Companies know that if they help their employees move up in the Knowledge Ranking, so they are more concerned about their personal information, they are unlikely to be of much help in securing the corporate data they are entrusted with.

GER: these sentences contradict each other

SHAYNE: Not sure what the hell happened there.

BOOK: Carole Cadwalladr doesn't use morals or ethics in her writing

GER: check with your lawyers

I think Ger might have saved me a lawsuit there… and I was so careful to not write in definitives… no always or nevers and no statements like this without a footnote and a ton of evidence of a claim.

Thank you Ger!

YOUR NEXT MOVE

It is our sincerest hope that you learned enough about the threats that you are exposed to, that your Knowledge Ranking has moved at least a letter or two up toward a B or an A.

Remember that the Weakest Link Scale is not about making you an A, it is about helping you move closer to an A by learning more about the threats so you can respond to them accordingly. Your Response Rank can be a 2, 3, or 4 and you can live a peaceful happy life exposing yourself to whatever threats you deem acceptable but in a more secure manner.

If you choose to have a Response Rank of 1 or 5, you are prepared to deal with stress that I don't understand. As a 1, you don't want to see or talk to anyone online, and maybe in the real world as well. I am an extrovert, so this makes no sense to me. As a 5, you will be dealing with insurmountable levels of stress from resetting passwords constantly and telling all your friends that your account was hacked… again.

That would get old fast, for you and your friends. Your boss might not let it get old.

Charles and I had a wonderful time researching everything for this book and I look forward to including the Weakest Link Scale in my future public speeches, presentations, and workshops.

Remember that our goal was not just about changing your strategies and tactics as you face the online threats that are out there, but it's also about changing your mindset. We want to change how you approach the perils of the internet with an overall goal of protecting your personal information in this digital world.

> This book is not just about changing your strategies and tactics, but it's also about changing your mindset.

At the end of the day, if you change your mindset, and increase your Knowledge Ranking, you will be well on your way to NOT be the weakest link in the protection of your personal data.

PLAY ALONG

Task A-1 Read the Book Again.

Please read the book again and take notes if you think you learned anything about securing your personal information. Writing the notes will help you retain the information while you implement it into your daily habits.

Bulk sales and personalized editions of the book can be yours by discussing options with the team at Kawali Publishing. You can contact them at www.KawaliPublishing.com where we practice extreme flexibility for everything from book club purchases to corporate sponsored editions.

Task A-2 Buy the Workbook

Purchase the companion workbook to take notes and save all the lessons that you learned from the book. This can be purchased from the www.DBTWL.com website by clicking on "Store".

We hope to be providing a package discount so that you can buy another book and workbook as a package and give away your first book. Watch the DBTWL website for updates.

Task A-3 Leave a Review

Please leave a review on your favorite store's website. Reviews on Google, Apple, Amazon, Goodreads, etc. will help other people find this book so they can start their journey on the Weakest Link Scale. If you don't have accounts on these sites, please leave a review on our website at www.DBTWL.com.

Task A-4 Join the Conversation

If you already have a Facebook account, join the DBTWL group and share your thoughts on this documentary, the book, everything you have learned.

http://footnote84.dbtwl.com

Task A-5 Follow us on Social Media

And please sign up for notifications and newsletters (not sent often) on the www.DBTWL.com website. Then look for us on your favorite social media platforms.

When I say follow "us", I clearly mean follow me, Shayne Kawalilak, the book Don't Be the Weakest Link, our publishing company at www.KawaliPublishing.com and my speaking career if you are interested, at www.RedFlagIT.com but what I do not mean… is follow Charles and I on social media, because there is no Charles on social media.

Task A-6 Remember that you know a public speaker now!

If the opportunity ever appears to you, make sure that you remember that you know a public speaker. You can see everything that I do on www.RedFlagIT.com or www.ShayneKawalilak.com (which still go to the same site at the time of publication but at one point in the future, they will split off).

Thank you for your time and we sincerely hope that you enjoy your adventure with the Weakest Link Scale and the book, Don't Be the Weakest Link: How to Protect Your Personal Information in a Digital World.

AUTHOR BIO – CHARLES ********

What can I say? Charles didn't want his last name on the cover. He certainly didn't want anything personal at the back of the book.

I cannot confirm that Charles is a man or a woman. I cannot confirm where he lives (but it's not the same city as me).

I can tell you three things about Charles-with-no-last-name. He is real, I have never called him Charles, and he might be in the witness protection program.

AUTHOR BIO – SHAYNE KAWALILAK

Shayne Kawalilak is a writer, teacher, and tech enthusiast with over 25 years of experience as a "professional geek." Happily married to his ex-wife, Shayne lives in Alberta, Canada, where they raised their nine children. When he's not diving into his passions for technology, writing, and public speaking, he dedicates his time to teaching, volunteering for causes close to his heart, and enjoying life with his family.

His love of storytelling and knack for making complex ideas accessible shine through in all his work. In rare moments of respite, Shayne can be found relaxing on a boat or swaying in a hammock, embracing the quiet joys of Alberta's natural beauty.